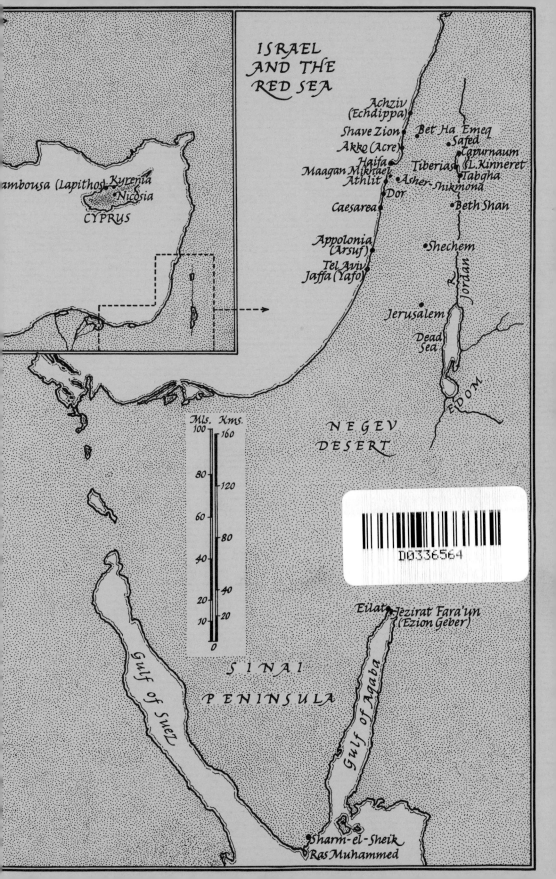

SECRETS

of the

BIBLE SEAS

AN UNDERWATER ARCHAEOLOGIST
IN THE HOLY LAND

by

Alexander Flinder

Foreword by

Magnus Magnusson

SEVERN HOUSE PUBLISHERS

First published 1985
by Severn House Publishers Ltd
4 Brook Street, London W1Y 1AA

Endpaper map by Denys Baker
Typeset by Nene Phototypesetters, Northampton
Printed and bound in Great Britain
by Butler & Tanner, Frome

British Library Cataloguing in Publication Data
Flinder, Alexander
Secrets of the Bible Seas:
an underwater archaeologist in the Holy Land
1. Underwater archaeology – Palestine
2. Palestine – Antiquities
I. Title
956.94   DS111.1

ISBN 0–7278–2047–8

Contents

Author's Note

My thanks to all those friends, archaeologists and divers, named and unnamed, who are part of this narrative. I am indebted also to Kendal McDonald for his early encouragement, to Rabbi Dr Louis Jacobs for his helpful advice, to Leonard Wolfson, David Young, and J. Kennedy Leigh, and Uri Kellner whose charitable trusts assisted our expeditions, and to Dr Moshe Dothan and Dr Avraham Biran for their permission to work on the various sites. My indebtedness also to Innes Rose and Vanessa Holt for their untiring advocacy, and to Julian Mannering for his patient guidance. Finally, my thanks to Dr Robert Stieglitz for his source material, to my daughter Barbara Flinder for her invaluable assistance in preparing the graphics and to Pamela Armstrong and Luise del Torto who typed and re-typed the manuscripts.

Foreword

I am the daughter of Earth and Water,
And the nursling of the Sky;
I pass through the pores of the ocean and shores;
I change, but I cannot die.

These evocative lines from Shelley's *The Cloud* have always symbolised for me the quintessence of underwater archaeology. 'I pass through the pores of the ocean and shores' – yes, it's almost as if archaeological remains on the seabed had actually grown there instead of being deposited there. 'I change, but cannot die' – yes, that's what archaeologists say about all artefacts and organisms: the traces are there, however minute, if only we know how and where to find them.

It's the finding that's fun. And nowhere, it seems, is the fun of finding more delightful, more beguiling, than underwater – especially under the pellucid summer waters of the Mediterranean. There, the pleasure of being in and under the water is a joy in itself, greatly heightened by the awareness of history submerged all around you.

This chummy, cheerful book by Alex Flinder, one of the pioneers of maritime archaeology in Britain, captures all the charm of the chase underwater. He is above all an enthusiast, a man who only discovered his true self, his true vocation, almost, when he yielded to an atavistic compulsion to start guddling around under water; and his enthusiasm has been given point and invaluable purpose by being harnessed to the service of archaeology.

9

His particular enthusiasm is for Biblical archaeology underwater – diving with a waterproofed Bible in hand, as it were. It was in that connection that I first met him, when I was researching a book and BBC television series on the Archaeology of the Bible Lands. Alex had been exploring around the picturesque coral island of Jezirat Fara'un in the Gulf of Aqaba, which scholars wanted to identify as the Biblical maritime base of Ezion-geber from the reign of King Solomon. And I wanted to know what he had found.

He didn't pontificate. He didn't insist that he had found 'proof' of the rather suspect Biblical account (there is no evidence, anywhere, of the legendary wealth attributed to Solomon's reign in the Old Testament). Instead, he enthused about the pleasure of it all – 'the pleasure of sitting on its shore and imbibing the vibrations of history that emanate from its stones', as he puts it in this book. And that enthusiasm is enormously infectious.

Over the past twenty years, Alex Flinder has come across all sorts of fascinating phases of history underwater: a shipwreck of Carthaginian figurines of the goddess Tanit, which he interprets as an abortive attempt to reintroduce the ancient religion of Phoenicia from its Tunisian colonies; the great harbour built by Herod at Caesarea; the Napoleonic siege of Acre (now Akko); Roman fish-tanks on Cyprus . . .

The finds are notable enough in themselves. But it is the fun of the finding, the sociability, the good companionship, the headiness of achievement, the thrill of discovery and recovery of things long-drowned – that's what this engaging book is all about.

Magnus Magnusson

Preface

Although archaeology of the underwater and coastal variety is my spur, I have not written, as it were, solely on this subject, but rather on the great pleasures that this activity has brought me, and in particular of the many years of fulfilment and interest derived from a personal involvement in exploring under the seas and on the shores of Bible Lands.

I was fortunate to have begun my formal diving in those days when the aqualung first came to be used as a tool of archaeology. All over the world divers were beginning to discover wrecks and submerged sites of archaeological and historical importance. The development of a new discipline and its integration into the total archaeological spectrum was, and indeed is still, a slow process. But out of the early stumbling years there has evolved a discipline which, although fairly mature in its philosophy and techniques, has yet to decide the name by which it is to be known. First baptised 'underwater archaeology', the purists soon preferred to be seen to be practising 'archaeology underwater'. But of course, we very soon realised that this description was too restricting; so it became 'marine archaeology'. This advanced to 'nautical archaeology' and later the term 'maritime archaeology' was coined. No matter – they all mean more or less the same thing; and if the reader catches me out using any one of these terms as a peg upon which to hang my hat, then he will appreciate my own unresolved confusion.

Writing about them is a way of reliving the many adventures that I shared with my colleagues on our expeditions; but in common with

11

land archaeology, field work represents only a small fraction of the time spent on a project. Every new discovery raises new problems, and the search for solutions continues in libraries among bookshelves and dusty archives. The heart can beat just as fast from a discovery revealed on the library table as it does from the uncovering of an artefact at a depth of a hundred feet.

Thus each and every one of the following chapters has its wet and dry episodes. But what continues to excite me is the realisation that so many of the questions generated by our discoveries, have yet to be fully answered. For example, from where did our Tanit figurines originate? And what is the mysterious shadow that lies forty feet beneath the sea bottom at Jezirat Fara'un in the Red Sea? Is there still more of King Herod's lost harbour at Caesarea remaining to be discovered; and what ancient treasures still lie beneath the shallow sands of the shores of Asher? My search continues, and I hope that this search will be taken up by divers and non-divers alike, as well as the archaeologist; for the sea bed and the sea shore is constantly changing; what was hidden yesterday is revealed today and what is glimpsed today is no longer there tomorrow. The reader will pose many questions for himself, and there are those who will query some of my conclusions. I hope that they do, for debate can only enliven research.

My chapters are 'in general' restricted to those sites upon which I have worked personally, or with which I have had some connection, and in attempting to convey the pleasure and excitement that I have derived from this work I have avoided the more esoteric aspects of research. For the reader, however, who wishes to delve deeper, I have compiled a bibliography of formal publications, and have also added the titles of books which will be of some help to those whose interest is stimulated.

I offer no excuse for having indulged myself equally in my love for history, for the Bible, for diving, as well as for archaeology, for each has played a part in my narrative and they are indivisible.

I

Beginnings

Gedi — Kenya

Hast thou entered into the springs of the sea? Or hast thou walked in the search of the depth?

JOB 38.16

My family and friends had cause for concern, and not without reason. After all, why should I, coming up to forty, suddenly put away my golf clubs and embark on a long and strenuous training course with people nearly half my age, purchase an aqualung and lots of rather odd looking equipment and take myself off to the coast to dive in cold and inhospitable waters? Why indeed?

I suppose that the answer to this question went back many years to the time of World War Two when I was posted to East Africa having been newly commissioned into the Royal Engineers. After some six months of training African Sappers on the dusty plains of Moshi below Kilimanjaro, I felt a need to get away and immerse myself in water; any

13

water, be it a pool, lake, river or sea; just to feel my body submerged. I had always been a keen competitive swimmer, so that in my teens a great deal of time had been spent in the pool. Water was the environment in which I was happiest, and such athletic prowess as I had achieved had been in water rather than on land. Moshi had left me physically and mentally dehydrated. A three-month stint in the Northern Frontier District desert of Kenya sinking a water well at Habaswein, which incidentally still exists, did little to abate my yearning.

Prompted by my Company Commander who said that he had 'Never seen a fella spend so much time under the shower', I confessed my craving. The CO was sympathetic. 'When your leave comes up old chap, take yourself off to Malindi.' I took his advice. In those far-off days, before the onslaught of post-war tourism, Malindi on the Indian Ocean shores of Kenya appeared nothing less than Shangri-la itself. The hot sun here on the coast seemed to be more kind. The warm broad beaches, gently cooled by soft breezes, and the transparent sea: this was Paradise to one who had known only the English Channel and the North Sea.

The one hotel at Malindi was run by a charming elderly couple, Commander Lawford, a retired naval officer, and his wife. After dinner on my first evening, the Commander introduced me to the Game Warden of the local coastal area. In my short time in East Africa, I had already met one or two wardens, and this fellow seemed to be the archetype of that breed. 'I gather that you are interested in seeing our reef,' he said. 'I'm going out in the morning; would you like to join me?' I replied that nothing would please me more. That evening in the bar I sat with the Commander and the Warden until the early hours listening to their stories of the Indian Ocean and of the fish and coral reefs, of fishermen and smuggling, early slave trading, and the history and customs of this fascinating Swahili coastline.

The next morning the Warden's outboard motor boat, manned by two African fishermen, carried the four of us through the surf and out to the offshore reef. 'Here you are,' said the Warden handing me a pair of goggles. They were only really two small glass semi-spheres held together with a piece of elastic. 'Put these on, they will help you to see better; and a word of warning, don't touch anything at all; some of the fish and coral here are really quite poisonous.' I dropped over the side of the boat, and lowering my head, peered beneath the surface. I shall never forget that moment; my first sight of a coral reef. Although I have, over the years, dived on some of the world's great reefs, that particular spot off Malindi will always claim a special place in my memory. It was my first experience of the world of the reef; a world of exquisite colour, form, movement and absorbing interest. Surely, of all life on Earth, that as lived on the coral reef must be among the most fascinating.

If the reef had been just the one gift that I was to receive from Malindi, then that would have been sufficient. But there was yet another to come; for during that first evening with the Commander and the Warden, they had spoken of a ruined city; the city of Gedi, some ten miles out of Malindi. Part of my architectural studies, which had been interrupted by the war, dealt with the history of architecture. This involved studying and drawing buildings of the various historical periods, and the part of this work I enjoyed most was going out and sketching, and measuring the actual buildings themselves, as distinct from learning about them from books. It occurred to me that Gedi might contain some material worth sketching. Besides, I wanted to see this mysterious place which I was assured by the hotel staff, was haunted by the spirits of those who had lived there. 'Do not go there by yourself Bwana,' pleaded my room servant. 'Take another Bwana with you.' Heeding his advice, I teamed up with the couple who occupied the next chalet to mine: a government telephone engineer and his wife.

As the three of us walked along the path which had been cut through the jungle leading to the ancient site, I began to understand the African's warning. The jungle had engulfed the stone-built city to such an extent that the trees had grown through the thick walls and houses had collapsed beneath the weight of dense growth. But as we went from building to building, and there were many, I somehow felt that if this place was indeed inhabited by spirits, then they were friendly spirits; at least they were friendly to me.

So it was that every afternoon after my swim on the reef, I would rest a little and then drive to Gedi to sketch and explore this ancient city.

I learned that it had been founded in the 15th century and although ordained an historical monument, the city had been studied little, and none of its buildings recorded. What a good idea, I thought, to record these for myself.

I was fortunate to have commenced my studies in those pre-war years when the sketchbook was considered an essential item of the architectural student's equipment. I am strongly of the opinion, and preach this dictum to my students, that the real way to appreciate a building is to draw it. One hour with a sketchbook is worth ten with a camera. How better, than with pencil and paper, can one attempt to understand the subtleties of a design, its setting, detail, proportion, and also its deficiencies?

Sketching has always been the most enjoyable of pastimes for me, and on occasions this pleasure has bloomed to something approaching ecstasy. So it was at Gedi. But it was here also that I first experienced the thrill of exploration, and something of a glimmer of what history is about. In those ten days at Malindi, I had evolved a formula for personal bliss. It was to swim the reef in the morning, followed by exploring and recording my ancient city in the afternoon. Then I would return to a cooling dip; 'toasties' and drinks on the verandah; good company for dinner and to close the day some Mozart from the Lawsons' old gramophone. To this day I cannot hear the E Flat Clarinet Trio without my inner ear recalling the background chorus of an African night, and the call of the surf along the edge of the Indian Ocean.

But this idyll had to end, and before long I was on my way to Burma via Ceylon and India. Other than a disastrous attempt to invent an underwater swimming apparatus during the crossing of the River Chindwin, I came through safely and my soldiering days with the Swahili-speaking Askaris of the Eleventh East African Division ended in 1945. I returned home to Trudie and we were married within the week. The next fifteen years were years of challenge and fulfilment, for these were the times of early struggle, of picking up one's studies where they had been interrupted five years earlier; finally qualifying and later starting a practice on my own account; and then our two children were born and grew up in the house that we built in the London suburb

16

of Highgate. But these years are only relevant to this particular story in that they sped by so very quickly, and I began to find myself restless.

I was forty and restless, a condition that I understand is all too common and by some accounts, perilous. I was rescued by, of all things, an announcement in the London *Times*. It read that in October 1962 there was to be held in London the Second World Congress of Underwater Activities. As I read on, I recalled from the deep recesses of my memory, that small reef at Malindi, so long ago. Nostalgia went with me to Church House in Westminster where the Conference was being held. My old army commander, Earl Mountbatten, who I had last met in the Burmese jungle, opened proceedings with tales of his own diving exploits, and I listened to those whose names are now part of diving history. Jacques Cousteau, Hans Hass, Jacques Piccard, Hannes Keller, Ed Link and so many others. Although I was not yet a diver, I responded to these people; I understood their passion, for I too, many years before, had experienced the magic world of which they spoke. A world beneath the oceans; the underwater world.

And then they came to the session which finally convinced me that I just had to learn to dive. The session was chaired by the eminent archaeologist Sir Mortimer Wheeler, and the subject was 'History Under the Sea'. I listened enthralled to one speaker after another, who told of discovering ancient wrecks on the sea bed; of those who were surveying sunken cities, and it was here that I first heard of that new science that was to play such a big part in my future life, 'Marine Archaeology'. The freshness of the subject was highlighted by Sir Mortimer who said, 'Up to date, I suppose that it is true to say that not a single underwater wreck has been completely excavated and fully recorded.' It was clear from those to whom I spoke between the sessions that the development of marine archaeology was indeed in its infancy, and as for Britain? Well, as one delegate put it, 'I can't think of more than three or four people in the whole country who have any experience at all on the subject.'

With some hesitation, I approached Sir Mortimer during the lunch break. We had met once briefly, but I did not think that he would remember. To my surprise he responded. 'Of course I remember you

17

my dear fellow; what are you doing here?' I told him of my interest. 'Absolutely splendid,' he replied. 'And with your skills you are just the sort of fellow they need,' Whereupon, he turned to a person near him calling, 'Joan my dear, I have a new recruit for you.'

Joan du Plat Taylor struck me as being a surprisingly mature lady to be one of the leaders of underwater archaeology, but it was not long before I realised why this was so. Her enthusiasm was infectious and I fell a willing victim to her persuasive charm. A professional archaeologist, Joan was the Librarian at the Institute of Archaeology in London. Being one of the first land archaeologists to realise the importance of underwater work, she had set about, with a few others, putting this new discipline on to a sound footing. The archaeological establishment had yet to be persuaded that underwater excavation was practicable; and there was the problem of divers who had to be diverted from 'treasure hunting'. The advancement that has been made in these areas is in no small way due to Joan du Plat Taylor's groundwork. She can surely claim to be the mother of marine archaeology in this country. For me, my subsequent meeting with Joan at her Institute was a formative one. 'First,' she said, 'You must learn to dive with the British Sub-Aqua Club; my branch at Holborn should suit you well.' She continued, 'As you are an architect, to start with harbours should be right for you; few people know much about ancient harbours; yes, harbours it shall be. What do you say to that, Alex?' It seemed that I had little choice. 'Right, Joan,' I replied. 'Harbours it shall be – to begin with.'

So this was how I came to be motoring to Cornwall with my family for a weekend's diving with the Holborn branch of the British Sub-Aqua Club. My involvement with the BS-AC has been a long and personally rewarding one. After a time I became the Club's Honorary Secretary, a job that I did for five years, and then I was the National Chairman for three years and now I am one of its Vice-Presidents. In common with many divers, I found that, whereas diving in itself is an exhilarating sport, comparable with skiing or rock climbing, diving with a purpose is more fulfilling and lasting, and my purpose was to use diving as a means to explore and seek history under the sea.

Thus marine archaeology had become my spur, and the years that followed took me around Britain and throughout the Mediterranean and further, diving on wrecks and submerged land sites, attending conferences and symposiums and meeting kindred spirits from all parts of the world who were engaged in this new and absorbing science. But I had yet to come to the Lands of the Bible.

II

The Lands of the Bible

*Ye that go down to the sea, and all that is therein; the isles,
and the inhabitants thereof.*

ISAIAH 42.10

It was February 1963 and we were on an El Al flight to Israel. It was
Trudie's birthday, and any illusion of a private toast was instantly
dispelled as I began to pour the champagne from the half-bottle. I felt a
nudge from the passenger next to me; 'Excuse me, is it a celebration?'
'Well – er – yes,' I replied, 'It's my wife's birthday.' 'Oh that's nice, and
you're taking her to Israel for her birthday?' I nodded. 'Sidney,' she
called, reaching across the gangway with her other elbow, 'Sidney, did
you hear, it's the lady's birthday and he's taking her to Israel as a
present, isn't that nice?' Sidney, who had topped his brandy with
ginger ale, raised his glass high and called across 'A Happy Birthday
my dear; l'chaim.'

The very large man in the row in front wearing a white shirt and rolled-up sleeves, with a big bushy beard and a skullcap, turned around, leaned on the back of his seat and stared down intently first at Trudie and then at me. Inclining his head to Trudie, and in what I am sure was intended as a confidential benediction he declaimed, 'Muzeltov,' (Good Luck) – but in a voice of such operatic sonority that it must certainly have reverberated right through to the flight deck. When all the responding muzeltovs in the nearby seats had died down, he then addressed me in the same confidential manner. 'Your first visit to Eretz Yisrael?' (the Land of Israel). I nodded. He pondered for a moment with one hand on beard; 'Believe me my friend, it will not be the last,' and then his face broke into a cherubic grin; he gave me the largest of knowing winks, turned and sat down.

Our amiable companion's declamation proved prophetic, for since then I have returned to Israel annually, sometimes twice a year, and my devotion to that country and its people has matured commensurately. But it has been an emotional involvement, for to attempt an understanding of modern Israel is to attempt the impossible. He who is devoted to this country must be prepared for anything and everything: For happiness and for sorrow; for refinement and coarseness; for great fulfilment and yet constant exasperation.

Our first two weeks in Israel were stimulating, frequently moving, now and then hilarious and finally exhausting, and we were thankful for the extra week that I had arranged to get in some diving at Eilat and to meet some underwater researchers whose names had been given to me by Joan du Plat Taylor.

Eilat, poised at the very end of the Gulf of Aqaba, one of the two slim fingers that terminate the north of the Red Sea, still retained in those days much of the ambience of a frontier town. The Eilatans, both men and women, had that pioneer look about them, and in the eyes of other Israelis the people and the town of Eilat was, as they often said, 'Something special'. This was a phrase that I was to hear constantly in Israel. It was always accompanied by hand-talk embellishment which emphasised the grade of the phrase – anything from the raising of the forefinger to throwing the head back with arms lifted high aloft.

Our hotel, the Queen of Sheba, maintained a small diving school run by Norberto Schlien, an immigrant from Brazil. Norberto seemed little impressed by my British Sub-Aqua Club logbook, although my logged dives appeared to have a slightly better effect. He explained diffidently that although he had indeed heard of the BS-AC, I was in fact the first British diver that he had met in Eilat and he hoped therefore that I would not mind 'Being put through a little test' during our dive. I replied that I thought his request prudent and we took ourselves off for a gentle amble of a dive over some nearby shallow corals.

I recalled that small reef at Malindi some twenty years before, for here were the same fish and the same corals; indeed, it was the same ocean, for the Red Sea is just a small segment of the tropical Indian Ocean. 'You like the sea here?' asked Norberto after the dive. 'Wonderful,' I replied, adding, 'Did I pass?' He looked at me curiously and put his hand on my shoulder, 'I think, Alex, that maybe you were testing me as well . . . ?'

The next day our plan involved a deep dive, about ninety feet or so. To avoid the need for decompressing on the way up, we decided to plummet straight down and then stay on the bottom only just as long as our dive tables permitted, round about twenty minutes. Our goal was *The Sinai*, a large wooden fishing boat that had sunk in a storm a few years before. Since then *The Sinai* had become a home for many creatures of the sea and was, as Norberto assured me, 'Something special'. It was certainly that, for as it lay at an angle on its side, *The Sinai* was the epitome of every child's picture of a deep-sea wreck. Sunken wrecks seldom fit the popular concept, but this one did. Although the ravages of the sea had begun to eat into its fabric, the vessel had remained surprisingly complete and even the mast was intact and upright. Festooned with marine growths, the wreck was alive with the constant activity of shoals of fish that glided in and around, and a group of large, stealthy barracuda passed us as we balanced on the tilted deck.

It was a thrilling dive but our time passed all too quickly, and when I checked my pre-set watch I saw that we had only about five minutes left. I looked over at Norberto who was lying on the deck looking down through an open hatch into the hold. Lifting his head he beckoned me to follow, and pulled himself forward and down into the black interior. I must admit that I do not like dark enclosed spaces under the sea, and I was therefore disinclined to follow. But Norberto's head popped up above the hatch and he beckoned me again impatiently. I had no alternative, so keeping close behind I pulled myself gingerly through the opening, and having felt for the ceiling of the hold just beneath the deck, there I stayed.

Norberto had gone deeper and I wondered why he had not switched on his torch, when suddenly its beam illuminated the bottom of the hold revealing one of the most scaring sights that I have ever seen – the swaying heads of six large Moray eels reaching up towards us, their enormous jaws opening and shutting ravenously. I had met Morays before, although never in these numbers, and I had always been assured by those who really knew, that these creatures were quite timid and only attacked when annoyed. This lot looked positively enraged.

Having no desire to linger, I turned, maybe a little too impulsively, to swim back out of the hold, and in so doing the buckle of my weightbelt caught against the side of the hatch. Before I could stop it, the buckle opened and eighteen pounds of lead slipped down past my legs smack into the Morays. The effect of this, coupled with the fact that my tank had less compressed air in it and had now become buoyant, was that I suddenly began to rise rapidly. In desperation I somehow managed to somersault over, and finning downwards like mad, reached towards the hatch opening. I just managed to grasp the edge, and with a heave tucked myself beneath the deck where I had been just a few moments before. Norberto had seen that something was wrong and was at my side in a moment. I pointed to my waist and then downwards. We both understood the situation; it would be crazy for him to try retrieving the weightbelt from among the Morays. He signalled that he was going off to find something heavy. I nodded and indicated that I would stay put. I had no other choice.

In Norberto's absence I pondered my predicament. Thankfully, I had stopped myself from rising, for an uncontrollable accelerating ascent from a depth of ninety feet would have meant a terrible risk of an embolism – a burst lung. As Norberto was still fully weighted, we could have surfaced holding on to each other, but it is better to find a compensating weight. On the other hand, there was the problem of the

23

agitated Morays just below me; that weightbelt crashing down on their heads could not have pleased them one bit. Thank heavens Norberto reappeared in time with a large rock. Detaching my grip from the edge of the hatchway I got up to him and gripped both of his shoulders. We pushed off gently from the depths and rose slowly to the surface ninety feet above us.

'Not a word about this to Trudie, Norberto.' He grinned. 'Have a good dive, you two?' Trudie called from the hotel terrace. 'Oh yes,' replied Norberto, 'You know Trudie, that dive was really something special.'

The next day we flew back to Lod Airport, and then drove on to Maagan Michael, a kibbutz on the shores of the Mediterranean south of Haifa. Here lived a man whom I very much wanted to meet. His name was Elisha Linder, and he was the Director of the Undersea Exploration Society of Israel. We arrived at the kibbutz and were welcomed by Elisha and his charming American-born wife Pnina as though we had been lifelong friends. Elisha and I took to each other immediately. It marked the beginning of a lasting friendship and partnership which I hope is reflected in these pages; for much of what I relate belongs to Elisha as much as it does to me.

Elisha showed us with pride the Society's small but beautifully set up museum and its diving centre, and then we drove eight miles south to Caesarea, the site on which Elisha and his group were currently diving. I recalled Caesarea from Rose Macaulay's *The Pleasure of Ruins*, but I was still unprepared for the extraordinary visual impact that this place made on me. The four of us sat in the uppermost seats of the recently excavated Herodian theatre, and before us the broken remains of the 'Logeion' – the stage – was silhouetted black against the red setting sun. Elisha told us of his plans. 'Beneath that sea,' he said, 'lies history that goes back to pre-Biblical times; it is there just waiting to be discovered. Alex, my dear friend, please come and help us. After all, the British have a long tradition of exploration and archaeology in the Holy Land. So is it not right that you should come here to work and continue in that tradition?' Elisha was very persuasive, and I needed little persuasion.

Within a few months I was back again in Israel with Elisha and Dr Joseph Shaw, an American archaeologist who was working on the sunken city of Kenchrea in Greece, and to whom Elisha had extended a similar invitation. The three of us teamed up to carry out a reconnaissance of various coastal sites which Elisha had listed as possibilities for future research.

Underwater archaeology was experiencing the same teething problems in Israel as it had met in other countries. The pattern was familiar; the archaeological establishment was not yet convinced that underwater sites were capable of being surveyed and excavated scientifically, on a par with land projects. It was necessary to demonstrate to them how this sort of work could fit into the general archaeological spectrum. In this respect Elisha had already done a great deal to smooth the path.

We were invited to a meeting at the Hebrew University in Jerusalem, and Joe gave an excellent lecture about his work at Kenchrea, demonstrating how it was possible to survey accurately under water. I spoke of the developing nature of marine archaeology in the United Kingdom; of the formation of the Council for Nautical Archaeology and of our plans for the protection by law of historic wrecks and sites, and of the progressively cooperative relationship between professional archaeologists, amateur divers, technologists and museums.

Having spent a couple of days lobbying the academics in Jerusalem, Elisha then took us off for ten days' diving and walking the potential sites. We went back to Caesarea, and then northwards to Dor, where Phoenician, Hellenic, Roman and mediaeval remains lie in the surf and straddle the beaches. To Athlit, with its ancient harbour remains and its majestic ruined mediaeval banqueting hall, recalling the Crusader kingdom at its zenith. Then further north to the town that must surely have one of the most romantic silhouettes in the Middle East – Akko, once known as Acre. Akko, with its small harbour nestling beneath the massive city walls and its domes and minaret poised delicately above deeply shadowed alleyways, has always been one of my favourite Middle-Eastern cities.

Then we went to the ancient town of Achziv, which the Bible tells us of being the city where the Hebrew Tribe of Zebulan dwelt among the Canaanites. Leaving the Mediterranean we drove eastwards, passing near Bet Ha-Emek, a kibbutz which Trudie and I had visited on our earlier trip and where we had watched a game of cricket played by

English emigrants on the most English of village greens, and then taken afternoon tea with marmalade and marmite sandwiches. Then we made a short stop at Safed, a magical old town with its narrow twisting alleys steeped in mediaeval mysticism, a place that reminds me so much of the hill towns of Tuscany; and finally on to Lake Kinneret, the biblical Sea of Galilee. One does not need to be of that faith to appreciate why this special water means more to the Christian than any other sea on Earth, and I understood what Joe meant when he said, 'Here, when you sit on the shore and meditate, it is not difficult to feel His presence.'

But our time was limited to just an overnight stay at Tiberius and then at dawn on the next day, we started our journey south, skirting the Dead Sea and on through the Negev Desert via the Kings' Highway of the Bible, and down to Eilat. It was good to be back there again and to meet for the first time Willi Halpert, who founded the Aquasport Diving Centre at Eilat's Coral Beach. With Willi and David Friedman, the Marine Biologist, now Curator of the Underwater Observatory and Aquarium in Eilat, we had three days of the most glorious and instructive diving, and I shall always be indebted to these two stalwarts for the example that they have shown to generations of Red Sea divers.

Between dives and in the evenings, Elisha, Joe and I summed up the results of our reconnaissance, and it was interesting to compare the impressions that the journey had made on each of us. Elisha was absorbed with the problems of setting up marine archaeology as a fully accepted discipline in Israel, and in inviting interest and participation from overseas experts. How well he ultimately succeeded in his aims since then is epitomised in the Department of Maritime Studies at the University of Haifa, which Elisha established and of which he was its first chairman.

Joe saw everything through the eyes of a scholarly field archaeologist; clinical and highly selective; anxious to direct effort with discretion into areas in which this new discipline could add to knowledge where conventional land methods were inadequate. My contribution to our discussions was mainly on logistics and organisation, but inwardly I was becoming aware of a mounting excitement that as yet I was unable to interpret objectively. Our journey had recalled names of places that had been familiar to me from the Bible, but they were names that I had known only in religious terms; obscure names like Edom and Beth Shan, and Shechem. But now I had actually visited these places and I began to find myself putting them into some sort of historical context. The Bible was beginning to come alive for me and I found it fascinating. On my earlier trip I had bought a small pocket Bible in Jerusalem; I thought that it might be a nice thing to have, but now I actually found myself reading it, and what is more, with some understanding.

But what really excited me was the realisation that the Bible was going to be an essential ingredient of our research, for how was it possible to explore the seas of the Bible without the Book itself? Biblical archaeology has been an established discipline for well nigh a century; was it now fanciful for us to be thinking of biblical marine archaeology? It sounded a little ludicrous, to say the least, but what if we were successful in achieving underwater discoveries of the Bible period? Surely it was only a matter of time.

There was an added aspect to the work that we were planning that did not really jell with me until I had been back home for a few weeks. Olga Tufnell, the archaeologist who had worked in Palestine in the thirties, had heard of our plans and suggested to me that the Library of the Palestine Exploration Fund was the most likely place for source material. It was that and more, for this small library, which is housed in two rooms of no great size in Marylebone, was to become the inspiration of all my future thinking on this subject. For here are contained the annals of the exploration of the Holy Land, from the earliest of days up to the present time. And it was here that I first read of the Golden Age of exploration, the 19th century, and of the giants of that period there was Conder, the leader of the PEF's splendid survey of Western Palestine; Dr Robinson, the great American explorer, whose *Biblical Researches in Palestine* earned him the Gold Medal of the Royal Geographical Society and George Adam Smith, the author of the classic *Historical Geography of the Holy Land*; and many others.

These were among those whom I came to admire and respect. And then there were the books I grew to love like Kinglake's *Eothen*; David Roberts' *The Holy Land* – surely one of the great classics of travel illustration; and *The Rob Roy on the Jordan* by William MacGregor, the inveterate canoeist who paddled his small craft from the source of the River Jordan to the Sea of Galilee, and then all around that inland lake.

These explorers, the forerunners of the archaeologists of the 20th century, had between them traversed every inch of the Holy Land. Well not quite. To be more precise one should say, all the lands that were above sea-level, for all these adventurous explorers had, without exception, been hindered by one disability: they did not possess the means of continuing their journey through to the floors of the oceans. The discovery of an ancient wreck on the sea bed was beyond their wildest ambitions, and even the stonework of sunken harbours and archaic submerged buildings were beyond their reach. Not that this prevented them from trying. Major Conder, in attempting to map the sunken remains of the Harbour of Sidon, recalled that 'The exploration had to be conducted in a novel manner; by swimming.' And MacGregor, excited by submerged stone blocks in the Sea of Galilee wrote, 'For seven hours a day during seven days my sight was half below and half above the surface, scanning every object with eager interest, and few searches are more exhaustive of time, patience and energy than this if it be done carefully . . . Thus eyeing the deep I began to examine the ruined wall, and to probe with my paddle.' The remains of the ancient harbour at Tyre so enthralled a Monsieur de Bertou, that his companion Dr Wilde, the father of Oscar Wilde, wrote in his travel diaries that his friend 'has prevailed on the Government to send out a diving bell to explore these submarine ruins.'

The prospect that now stimulated me beyond measure was that we, with the aid of the aqualung, were now planning to continue with the exploration of the Holy Land, where all those who had gone before us had been forced to halt. On reflection, I suppose that this was a little arrogant, but it did reflect my hopes at the time and, as it turned out, we did, over the years, make a number of fascinating and even important discoveries.

What follows is my personal account of some of these discoveries that we made beneath the seas and on the shores of the Lands of the Bible.

III

The Goddess from the Sea

Their land is also full of idols; they worship the work of their own hands that which their own fingers have made.

ISAIAH 2.7

The telephone rang. The caller was my old friend Arie Ben Eli, the Director of the Maritime Museum of Israel. 'Alex, I have with me some very interesting photographs that I would like to show you, but I'm on my way to New York and am only stopping in London overnight; can we meet?' A few hours later we sat in a restaurant overlooking the Serpentine in London's Hyde Park, and Arie handed me a set of photographs. They were of a group of terracotta figurines about six inches high, and each was of a woman standing on a base. On the base of one of the figurines was inscribed a dolphin, and on another a strange sign that rather reminded me of the Egyptian Ankh. Its form was of a circle which sat on a horizontal arm balanced over a triangle.

Arie told me how he came to have these figurines. Just a few days before, an old acquaintance of his had called on him at the Museum in Haifa. Robbi Shosmos, for that was his name, was a fisherman from Akko, and also a part-time diver. Arie was rather surprised to receive this caller for, in common with most fishermen, he was more disposed to avoid the attentions of archaeologists than invite them. However, on being asked the purpose of his visit, Shosmos produced from his pocket the figurines that were the subject of the photographs. He said that he had found them in the sea off Shave Zion, a small seaside town between Akko and Naharia, and that if Arie was interested he would take some divers to the spot where he had found them. 'What is that English expression?' Arie asked, 'About a gift horse?' 'I see what you mean,' I replied. Arie continued his story. He contacted Elisha Linder, and on the following day a group of divers from the Undersea Exploration Society of Israel, accompanied Shosmos to Shave Zion, dived on the site and recovered two more figurines. Arie explained to me that all this had happened just before he left and that he had no time in which to research the material. But of one thing he was sure; figurines of this sort, he said, had never been found in Palestine. Would I, he asked me, see if the British Museum could help in identification.

I phoned the British Museum immediately and made an appointment for the following morning. Next day, after taking Arie off to Heathrow Airport, I went on to the British Museum to see Dr Richard Barnett. Dr Barnett, whom I knew as the Chairman of the Anglo-Israel Archaeological Society, was the Keeper of the Western Asiatic Department of the British Museum. He studied the photographs intently. 'Found in the sea you say, and off the coast of Israel?' I nodded. He examined the photographs even more closely with a magnifying glass. 'Do they mean anything to you?' I asked. 'And what about that strange sign?' 'What indeed,' replied Dr Barnett. 'That sign, if I'm not mistaken, is what is sometimes known as the Enigmatic Sign of Tanit – the Goddess of Carthage.' And then suddenly he jumped up from his chair and hared off through the door beckoning me to follow him. His assistant and I followed hot on his heels. 'It's not often he gets as excited as this,' she said breathlessly, as we sped first through the gallery marked Roman and Coptic Period in Egypt, into the Egyptian

Early Dynastic gallery, and then the Pre-Dynastic Period, finally stopping at the gallery marked Phoenicia and Carthage.

Dr Barnett recovered his breath, and then pointing at a headstone in a corner, exclaimed, 'There is your sign – the Sign of Tanit.' I bent down and examined the stele closely and compared the sign with that on the photograph which I had hastily picked up as we dashed from Dr Barnett's study. Yes, it was the same; a circle on a horizontal bar on a triangle. And then Dr Barnett drew my attention to other stelae where the sign was repeated, sometimes with variations, but they were all still quite recognisable. I recalled what Arie had told me about these figurines being totally unknown in Palestine. I put this to Dr Barnett, adding that I knew of the Canaanite-Phoenician gods Baal and Astarte in the Eastern Mediterranean, but what, I asked, was this Carthaginian goddess doing on the coast of ancient Phoenicia? 'What indeed,' replied Richard. 'It seems to me that you and your diver friends in Israel are going to have a very busy and interesting time finding out; I suggest that you start your research here and use our Library, and Carol Mendelsohn here will help you.'

I telephoned my secretary to tell her that for the rest of the day I could be reached at Dr Barnett's Library, and then told her to send this telegram to Arie in New York and to Elisha in Haifa – FIGURINES ARE OF TANIT STOP CARTHAGE STOP IMPORTANT FIND STOP. I did not appreciate at the time quite how important, but this began to emerge as I sat for the rest of the day ploughing through volume after volume of journals and papers that Carol had piled up on my desk. This briefly is what I learned about the Goddess Tanit.

The Phoenicians were a coastal people, and they occupied the narrow strip of coast that ran from what is now the southern border of Turkey down to somewhere south of Haifa. In the 9th century BC, Dido the Princess of Tyre, sailed to a small port of call in what is now Tunisia, and founded the Punic city of Carthage. The Phoenicians were the foremost seafarers of the biblical period, and they established many settlements throughout the Mediterranean: of these Carthage was the greatest, and although she developed independently through the centuries and flourished, the city never forgot her original link with Tyre. Back in the Tyrenian homeland, the ancient Canaanite gods Baal and Astarte were worshipped, but in Carthage these two deities took second place to the Goddess Tanit who was known as the Queen of Carthage.

So far so good, but the point that intrigued me as I read on was that each writer had emphasised that, whereas Tanit was generally known in the ancient western Mediterranean, there was no evidence at all of this Goddess having been worshipped in the east, that is in the Phoenician homeland. Indeed, the Sign of Tanit as such, was quite unknown in this area. It certainly seemed that what Arie had said was absolutely correct.

ONE OF THE VOTIVE FIGURINES OF THE GODDESS TANIT FROM THE SHAVE ZION WRECK SITE.

'You must be exhausted,' said Carol, as she appeared with yet another cup of coffee. 'You haven't moved from that desk all day.' 'I guess I am rather tired,' I replied, 'But do you know what, Carol? I'm beginning to think that our fisherman friend Robbi Shosmos, has made a pretty important discovery.'

The Goddess from the Sea

In the weeks that followed, Arie, Elisha and I became engaged in a stream of correspondence. The UESI Underwater Team had established that there was even more material on the sea bed spread over a fairly large area, and that a full scale underwater search and survey was necessary. I was invited to take charge of the survey and plotting operation, and on my arrival in Israel I found that Elisha had assembled an experienced team of divers. There was Yigal Shiloh, the archaeologist who is currently in charge of the excavations in the ancient city of David in Jerusalem. There was Shelly Wachsman, an archaeologist from the Hebrew University of Jerusalem, and our geologist was Yaakov Ovir from nearby Naharia. The photographer was Danny Birenbaum from Kibbutz Kabri; and our chief diver, Chia Edleman of Kibbutz Ramat Yohman, headed a group of remarkably energetic divers; Erik from Haifa, Booky from Ramat Gan, Yospe of Kibbutz Nachal Oz near Ghaza, and Menahem Heymann, and Chaim Serber. The Department of Maritime Stuides at Haifa University sent a group of students led by their tutor, Sara Aronson, who made it a family affair, camping on the beach with her husband and four children. Sara's husband, Avi, a building engineer, joined with me in the surveying operation. The laboratories at the Maritime Museum and at the Hebrew University offered their services for the conservation of finds, and Shosmos the fisherman rented us his boat together with his assistant, Idris Hathut, and one large Alsatian dog named Kelev, a veritable canine swimming champion who delighted in accompanying the divers whilst on the surface. Finally, we were joined by our expedition doctor to whom I made some feeble quip about hoping not to have need of his specialist services. 'I should hope not,' he replied, 'As a specialist I'm a gynaecologist!'

We were lucky in our location, for underwater sites are often a long way from common amenities, so that one either has the alternative of camping on the shore, or having a long daily drive from one's base. In this case, the site was less than a mile offshore from Shave Zion, which turned out to be a small resort township with pleasantly designed single-storey houses set in luxuriant, sweet-smelling gardens. Principally, the town was the centre of a Moshav, a communal farm settlement. Its name means Return to Zion, and it was founded in 1938 by a group of German-Jewish immigrants descended from generations of farmers and cattle merchants in the village of Wrexingem Wurtten-berg. A touching reminder of this was their small synagogue, a replica of the original which had been burnt down by the Nazis. Of archaeological interest on the shore, are the remains of a Byzantine church of the 5th century AD which has some striking mosaics.

Our operating base was the ground floor store of the municipal beach café, called appropriately the Neptune Restaurant. Here we stored our aqualungs and all the rest of the equipment, together with the air compressor, and our meals were taken in the upper level café under the matriarchal eye of Rachel, a very formidable lady who took it personally if anything edible was left on our plates. Those of us who were not within reach of their homes, were put up by local residents.

By the time I arrived, everything was ready to go; the survey base line had already been placed on the sea bed running due north-south from the spot on which the original finds had been made. I wasted no time in diving to see what sort of a terrain I had to deal with, and I found that the site was some thirty feet down – a pretty comfortable working depth – with a bottom of monotonous shallow corrugated gulleys, very typical of the many sandstone offshore reefs that run parallel with this coastline.

Our first job was to search and locate, and we instructed the divers that initially, under no circumstances, was anything at all to be lifted. What we wanted to do was to determine the spread of the material, whatever that material was, and the full extent of the site.

Having assessed the character of the site, I wanted to see what sort of material we were dealing with, and Elek, with whom I was diving, directed me towards a lump of jagged rock lying at the bottom of a gulley. There seemed to be nothing unusual about this rock, except that it was tinged with a sort of red vegetation. I lay on the bottom, my face just a few inches from the rock and ran my fingers over its contours to see if there was indeed anything unusual about it. I could detect nothing at all, and looked enquiringly at Elek, who then pointed at a spot lower down. I touched this area gently, then I could see what he meant; it was the small, curved edge of a piece of pottery. The ability to detect such aberrations comes naturally to some and is acquired by

34

others, but it is a skill that is essential to every underwater searcher. The more familiar one becomes with a terrain, the easier it is to detect the abnormality. Once it had been pointed out to me, I knew that this thin sliver of pottery I felt between my fingers, was the bottom edge of the base of a figurine. This fine sliver was all that one could see, but it was sufficient.

Our search continued day after day with three diving sessions in every day. Fresh teams of divers took over where others left off, and wherever pairs of divers discovered anything at all, they would mark this with a floating red bobbin, each with its individual number. After some days the sea bed looked quite bizarre, with literally hundreds of red bobbins floating about over a wide area. In fact, the range of material extended for some four thousand square yards and we certainly had our time cut out, accurately plotting the position of every find. As soon as we finished one group, the material was carefully prised from the bottom and lifted. So hard was this terrain, however, that on occasions we had to resort to hammer and chisel, and finally to drills operated from compressed air bottles.

Soon the limited space at the Neptune Restaurant was overflowing with plastic boxes and bags bulging with strange-looking pieces of rock, and we were offered the use of the local Community Centre as a store room and temporary laboratory and workshop. As the cleaning progressed we found that a great many of the finds were of our now familiar terracotta figurines. They appeared to be of three distinct sizes; there were those that were about six inches tall, and fairly coarsely modelled. Then there were others about twelve inches high with rather better modelling, and large ones about fifteen inches tall, these being the most finely modelled of all. We knew that our finds were important, but what really interested us was that without exception, all the figurines were of the Goddess Tanit; of this we were certain. The Sign of Tanit appeared nearly always though sometimes it was replaced by a dolphin and the figure of the Goddess herself was always recognisable. In all cases she was hooded, her left hand was held across her breast and the right invariably lifted in a salute of benediction.

At the conclusion of the expedition we had recovered more than three hundred figurines of various sizes from six to fifteen inches high and there were at least that number of broken fragments. This is the largest cache of this sort ever to have been recovered from beneath the sea and in addition there was a large quantity of pottery sherds including complete vessels, mostly amphorae.

VARIOUS FORMS OF THE SIGN OF TANIT.

Archaeological discoveries often pose more questions than they provide answers. In the case of the Shave Zion site we had a multitude of unanswered questions; an archaeological mystery of the first order. According to all scholarly opinion, Tanit was unknown in ancient Phoenicia and even when it was suggested that the Goddess may have had her roots there, no equivalent material to our figurines had ever been found on land. How, therefore, are we to explain the existence of this large quantity of Tanit votive figurines less than a mile offshore of the land in which she was a stranger?

It took me many years of research and some thousands of miles of travel to arrive at a possible solution, and in order to reach that stage there were many other questions to be answered.

First, what was the nature of our site? Elisha and I had already discounted any idea of this having been a land site which had subsided due possibly to an earthquake or some sort of techtonic movement. Our geologist pointed out that there was no evidence at all of subsidence to any degree in this area; and even if this was a possibility, why had not similar figurines been found on land at Shave Zion or anywhere else along the coast?

Having disposed of the land subsidence theory we concluded that our discovery represented the cargo of a wrecked ship. This theory was supported by the pottery and amphorae typical of that carried by ships of the ancient world. Following from this premise there was a further question – in which direction had the ship been going: towards ancient Phoenicia or from it? Surely not the latter, because the ship's cargo was unfamiliar to Eastern Phoenicia and therefore the ship must have come from the West and been making its way to one of the Eastern ports.

Second, what was the age of the wreck? The established method of dating most archaeological sites is by its pottery, and this we had in abundance. The amphorae were of the biconical type characterised by a long pointed toe, flat rim and small ringed handles. This type of amphora is fairly well known in both the eastern and western Mediterraneans and is dated from the 4th to 6th century BC.

A recapitulation of our conclusions so far was that we had a cargo of terracotta figurines of the Goddess Tanit from a ship of the 4th to 6th century BC wrecked on its way to the Phoenician homeland. But what of the ship itself: why did we find nothing of this? The answer is that the ship, having gone down in comparatively shallow waters onto a flat reef, would have broken up rapidly, and the likelihood of any timbers remaining intact at this shallow depth was remote. What remained was the terracotta cargo and pottery which had been spread by the surging and moving sea over a large area, and it is likely that the three hundred or so figurines that we had recovered must have been but a fraction of the ship's total cargo.

But there were some fundamental questions that still remained unanswered. Other wrecks found in the Mediterranean were generally of merchant ships carrying the usual cargoes of ancient maritime trade such as grain, wine, olives and ingots. But none of these commodities were found on this site, instead we had a cargo of votive figurines of the Goddess Tanit who was unknown in this area. Who was Tanit? What did she represent? And why had it been so important to allocate a whole cargo of a valuable ship to this Goddess and bring her to the Land of the Bible which was occupied by two peoples; the Phoenicians of Tyre and Sidon whose Gods were Baal and his consort Astarte, and the Israelites who worshipped but one God.

Tanit was the Goddess of the Western Phoenicians, and her home was in Carthage. It was therefore to Carthage that Trudie and I took ourselves in search of Tanit for the next stage of my quest. More precisely it was to Tunis that we went; for that modern city now stands on the site of its ancient counterpart. In 146 BC the conquering Romans destroyed Phoenician Carthage by having it systematically pillaged, burnt to the ground and ploughed over. In recent years, archaeology has begun to reveal some of the Punic remains and foremost among these is the Sanctuary of Tanit

The Sanctuary of Tanit is situated at Salammbo within two minutes walk of the site of the great harbour of Carthage. Within the entrance there is a flat, gravelled area on which stand hundreds upon hundreds of stelae of the type that I first saw in the British Museum; and everywhere engraved on the stelae is the Sign of Tanit in its various forms. These headstones had been transferred by the archaeologists from the grotto beyond, into which we then descended. In the undergrowth and under the trees, between the natural rocks and at all levels were more stelae. The path took us through to a dark, vaulted enclosure within which lay countless more of these small memorial tablets crowded together, lined against the walls protruding from the earth, some standing free and others fallen and broken.

It was to this Sanctuary that the Carthaginians went to pay homage to their Goddess. But the Sanctuary was more than just a place of worship, for the archaeologists had discovered beneath each of the stelae small earthenware pots containing the cremated remains of small children, most of whom were under two though some would have been as old as twelve years. The Sanctuary, which has not yet been fully excavated, has revealed thousands of these urns, final proof that the many stories of the Phoenicians' practice of infant sacrifice were only too true.

The Sanctuary of Tanit was, in fact, a sacrificial precinct, or Tophet. The Tophet is mentioned in the Bible in the Book of Jeremiah – 'they have built the high places of Tophet which is in the Valley of Hinnon, to burn their sons and their daughters in the fire which I commanded not, neither came it into my mind'. Indeed, archaeological evidence has now shown that the predominant and essential ingredient of Tanit worship was infant sacrifice and, furthermore, the strata of excavations at Salammbo show conclusively that this practice continued uninterrupted up to the time of the destruction of the city. The cruellest of times was when the State was under threat or attack when the Priests would command the populace to bring their little children to be cast into the fiery pit. The name Tophet was derived from the great din made with the drums (tophim) to prevent the father hearing the cries of his child as it was burnt. Although a work of fiction, Gustave Flaubert's epic novel *Salammbo* paints a vivid picture of the sacrifices at the time of the bloody war triggered off by Carthage failing to pay her mercenaries. A war which went on for three-and-a-half years and ended in 238 BC. The most touching memory that I have of Salammbo is of a small double stelae with two signs of Tanit – a memorial to twin infants.

In my continued search for Tanit I went in the following year to the tiny island of Motya which lies just offshore of western Sicily. Here again I came to a Tophet and in the small museum nearby the Sign of Tanit was repeated time and time again. Wherever the Carthaginians colonised the western Mediterranean there one will find the Tophet; at Nora in southern Sardinia, at several sites along the coast of north Africa and in Sicily where at Syracuse in 310 BC the sons of five hundred nobles were sacrificed when that city was faced with defeat.

It is quite clear that the practice of infant sacrifice to Tanit prevailed in western Phoenicia up to the time of that Empire's downfall and yet from all available evidence it would appear that infant sacrifice, which was a feature of Canaanite worship in the earlier biblical period, had disappeared in the eastern Phoenician homeland in the later centuries. The Canaanites and the Israelites of the Old Testament had both fought each other and lived side by side and there were times when their cultures and religious practices intertwined. The Phoenician Emperor Hyram of Tyre, joined with King Solomon in the building of the Temple in Jerusalem, and these two great monarchs cooperated in a joint maritime venture from Ezion Geber in the Red Sea. But throughout the whole of the Old Testament the Hebrew Prophets denounced the practices of Baal and the one practice they reviled above all was that of infant sacrifice. The Prophet Jeremiah condemns 'burning their sons in the fire as burnt offerings unto Baal'. In the Book of Leviticus we read, 'Thou shalt not let any of thy seed pass through the fire to Moloch.' And the Book of Micah laments the killing of the firstborn – 'shall I give my firstborn for my transgression, the fruit of my body for the sin of my soul?' By the 4th century BC, the likely date of the Shave Zion wreck, infant sacrifice in the Holy Land was a memory of the dim and distant past.

When one considers the Shave Zion wreck in the context of this history of infant sacrifice, one cannot avoid the extraordinary conclusion that our wreck must have represented a determined attempt not only to introduce the Goddess Tanit from western Phoenicia into the Phoenician homeland, but also the practice of infant sacrifice which was an essential part of her worship. What more conclusive proof can there be than the close examination of some of the Shave Zion figurines, for at the feet of the Goddess Tanit there is the unmistakable shape of a swathed infant.

Our figurine wreck represents, in my view, not a commercial cargo, but what must have been an act of political and religious significance. This theory was reinforced when I met up again with an old friend at a recent international conference. Mention any part of the globe and Bob Marx has dived there. 'I recently saw a paper that you did with Elisha Linder in the *Illustrated London News* on the Tanit figurine wreck,' said Bob. 'Well, it might interest you to know that a few years ago I dived on a wreck with exactly the same sort of cargo, outside Tyre in Lebanon, but in our case the figurines were buried in sand and we brought them out by the hundred.' Whereupon Bob produced some photographs of the figurines and they were indeed replicas of our own material. We now know that the 4th century BC Tanit invasion of the Phoenician homeland was carried out by certainly two ships and I would suspect even more.

What was the explanation for this invasion of religious ideals? We shall never know, but I should like to put forward an idea or two. We know that the Carthaginian colonies and the cities of Tyre and Sidon were always in close touch with each other. It was customary for emissaries to travel back and forth between the old and new countries. But whereas Carthage had retained the old fundamental religious beliefs, particularly that of infant sacrifice, the religions of Tyre and Sidon had become diluted from their close contact with the Israelites and then by their occupation by the Assyrians followed by the Babylonians and then the Persians. The cities had, over centuries, been successively influenced by these various cultures. By the mid 4th century Tyre and Sidon had been conquered by Alexander, and the old Phoenician culture, language and religion would all but have disappeared. But in Carthage and its colonies the old religions, albeit with their Punic adhesions, were at their zenith.

Is it not possible that the Tanit figurine wrecks at Shave Zion and the other at Tyre are evidence of an attempt by the Phoenician religious fundamentalists of the day to bring the peoples of the two cities back to the old ways?

One final thought: the two full ship loads – and there may have been more of the Tanit idols dispatched from the western colonies to the Phoenician homeland – failed to reach their destination; for in spite of over one hundred years' of archaeological excavation in the Holy Land not a single Tanit figurine has ever been found on land.

If the chroniclers of the Bible had known of these two ships, might we not today have read something like this in the Scriptures?

> 'And it came to pass that the sons of Baal made graven images and sent them in ships to the land, that once again their seed be made to pass through the fire to Moloch. And the Lord's wrath was great and the Lord sent out a great wind into the sea, and there was a mighty tempest in the sea so that the ships were broken and the false gods cast forth into the sea that they did not come into the land.'

IV

Island in the Red Sea

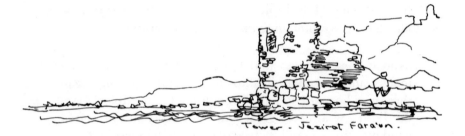

Tower - Jezirat Fara'un.

And King Solomon made a navy of ships in Ezion Geber, which is beside Eloth, on the shore of the Red Sea in the Land of Edom. And Hiram sent in the navy his servants, shipmen that had knowledge of the sea with the servants of Solomon. And they came to Ophir, and fetched from thence gold, four hundred and twenty talents, and brought it to King Solomon.

I KINGS 9, 26.28

Jezirat Fara'un; that is the name that I prefer and it is the name by which I shall always remember this island. But it has many other names; the Crusaders called it Isle de Graye, and our Sinai travellers of the 19th century also had their favourite names for this tiny island in the Gulf of Aqaba some ten miles south of Eilat. Burckhardt knew it as Koreye; Von Schubert preferred Kurayyah, and Arconati – Hezirat el Querigh. Rupell called it Emrag, and modern Israel – Coral Island.

42

Island in the Red Sea

Curiously my love affair with Jezirat Fara'un started many years before we had actually met. Our introduction was affected by David Roberts, the British artist who, having travelled through Palestine, Sinai and Egypt in the 1830s, published, with the assistance of the engraver Louis Haghe, his masterpiece, *The Holy Land*. My copy is the most prized volume on my bookshelf. I cherish all of Roberts' drawings, but the one that has always been my favourite is that of the island which he calls Isle de Graye. I am sure that Roberts himself must have had a particular affection for this place, for he used it as a setting for a self-portrait. The charming vignette in the foreground has Roberts dressed in native garb, as was the custom of Holy Land travellers in those days, putting the final touches to his sketch, while his dragoman waits with ill-disguised impatience, and even the camel appears indignant. The rest of the caravan, being less tolerant, has commenced the journey north towards Aqaba.

But in spite of my almost yearly diving visits to Eilat, the island, which was only some ninety minutes travel southwards, had been inaccessible, for whereas Eilat was in Israel, Jezirat Fara'un was in Egyptian Sinai. In those days, passage through the border was not permitted, and an approach to the island from the south would have meant a journey from Egypt nearly as arduous as Roberts' had been some hundred and fifty years earlier. Thus my visit to Jezirat Fara'un had remained an unfulfilled ambition; that is, until 1967 when the Six Day War ended with the occupation of Sinai by Israel. Three months later I happened to be in Israel visiting my son Harvey, who was working as a volunteer on Kibbutz Ma'agan Michael, the home of Elisha and Pnina Linder. But I would be less than honest if I did not admit that a secondary purpose of my visit was to see if I could, somehow or other, manage to visit the island that I had known only from books and photographs.

When I tentatively broached the subject with Elisha, he laughed and replied that he must have read my mind because he had, in fact, arranged, as a surprise, for a small group of us to drive south to Eilat and then on to Jezirat Fara'un for a short visit. In a few days, a small party consisting of Elisha, Harvey, myself and some of our old diving friends, was on its way driving at night through the Negev desert via the Aravah

– the biblical Road of the Kings – and south to the Red Sea. We stayed overnight at Eilat and then at dawn continued our journey southwards along the coastal road, whilst Harvey joined with Avremela to take all our heavy diving gear by boat.

Nowadays, with the new coastal road, this area has become accessible even to the cyclist, and tourism has, sadly, left its indelible marks. But in those days, as we left Israel's southern border it was as though we were slipping back in time, for Sinai and its eastern coastal strip had, in spite of centuries of historical occupation, remained virtually untouched. I felt as though I was in the footsteps of Roberts himself, and other explorers such as Palmer, who met his death here, and of Burkhardt and Burton.

But first there was the experience of traversing that obscenity of war with which I had been only too familiar in my earlier years – the anti-tank minefield. The narrow track marked by white tape, barbed wire and skull-and-crossbones signs, snaked through the minefield which had been laid in the no man's land between the two former borders. Although the track had been clearly defined, I was relieved when we reached the end of it and were able to continue safely on to Taba, the small oasis at which, since time immemorial, nomads had come to the water holes to graze their camels beneath the small clump of Sudanese date palms. To the botanist this particular group of palms is notable for being the most northerly of their species and their peculiarity is that, unlike the familiar single-trunk palm trees, they have multiple branches.

As we drove through this attractive oasis beside the turquoise sea, I was reminded of the period, at the beginning of this century, when Taba was the scene of a conflict that nearly sparked off a major war between the two great empires of the day, the British and the Turkish. This episode became known as the Taba Incident. The frontier between Turkish-ruled Palestine and British-supported Egyptian Sinai was ill defined, and the Turks, in search of better wells, ventured a few miles into what the Egyptians maintained was their territory. Military skirmishing commenced, and this threatened to develop into a serious conflict until sense prevailed and the two sides decided to get together and agree on a local Commission to settle the border once and for all.

The Egyptians appointed British officers to act on their behalf and, after a great deal of bargaining, the border was eventually delineated. The Turks appeared well satisfied with the Treaty which they thought had left them with many advantages; but their contentment soon turned to anger when they discovered that they had been duped. Unknown to the Turks, the most prolific of the watering places, that at Wadi Gedirat, had remained in Sinai territory. In 1915 the border was again adjusted under the direction of T E Lawrence and it is these two interpretations of the border which accounts for the Taba no man's land of today with the Israeli and Egyptian border posts very nearly looking over each other and the nine-storey Sonesta Hotel poised between.

After Taba we continued our drive along the rough coastal road, closely hugging the sea on our left and the Sinai Desert on our right, and I recall how at the time I revised my opinion of the Sinai traveller, Doughty, whose flowery style of writing I had always found difficult to accept. But now, as I experienced this Sinai landscape for the first time, I realised how inadequate everyday language is to portray a beauty such as this. The sea, a delicate and luminous hue of blue and green, and across the Gulf, the purple mountains of the Arabian Desert were entrancing. But above all, it was the utter silence and the stillness of the air that enraptured me.

In anticipation, I peered ahead for my first glimpse of Jezirat Fara'un, the island that I had known so well and had yet to visit; and then it came into view in the distance, a dark form rising as some creature from the deep sea. For a moment, it was obscured from view by a jutting headland, but as we rounded the bay we suddenly came upon it again in its full glory, and it was breathtaking. We halted the vehicle, stepped down and then sat on the beach in a state of awe, for this island was far more impressive than I had known it from photographs, and even my Roberts print had not fully done it justice. The close blending of the mediaeval building atop the island, completed a nobility of form such as I have seldom seen. Yet, as I was to learn, this was no static beauty, for I grew to marvel constantly at the way the island changes in its mood as the shades and shadows are remodelled minute by minute by the encircling sun. We sat on the beach and waited for the boat and the others to arrive, and we were all conscious that these were moments to savour. It was still quite early and the sun had not yet fully risen; the sea was touched by a slight breeze from the south, and not a soul or craft was to be seen other than our boat, still a speck on the horizon. We were alone with the island and the sea.

The few of us sat, with only now and then a whispered phrase of appreciation, until we heard the chugging of the outboard motor, and our inflatable boat with Harvey and Avremala, rounded the headland of the bay and made towards us on the beach.

Leaving our station wagon tucked into the shade of the cliff, we jumped into the boat and directed it towards the dark stone, circular tower facing us on the west side of the island. I could hardly contain myself as we stepped into the shallows and tied up the boat. I wanted to explore the island there and then, but our time was limited, and our main purpose on this first occasion, was to dive as soon as we could and explore the underwater environment around the island.

We changed hastily into our wetsuits, geared up and then snorkelled out a few metres from the shore and dived down to the sandy slope a few metres below. Avremala and Elisha remained in the inflatable to give us surface cover, and Yoske Galilee, Shuka Shapira, Harvey and I grouped together on the sea bed and looked around. Once again that familiar feeling came over me; as one who has entered a strange and unfamiliar world where Man is very much the visitor. A few days before, I had been diving in the Mediterranean where there were, alas, few fish to be seen. But here we were surrounded by myriads of coloured tropical fish of all shapes and sizes, while the water was warm and the visibility superb. We had previously arranged our dive plan, which was to encircle the island in a clockwise direction, and we split into pairs and commenced to fin slowly northwards. I had reason for slightly more than the normal caution that one should have on a new dive, because I had recently read a book which had only just that week been released from the Official Secrets List. It was a Royal Navy Intelligence Handbook on the Red Sea, and the chapter that described the island, contained the following passage: 'And the difficulty of sailing there in shark-infested, wind-troubled water, has kept all but a few visitors away for at least eight centuries.'

As it turned out, we did not see a single shark on that occasion, nor indeed have I come across any during my subsequent years of diving around the island. It was not until the following year when I first dived at Sharm el Sheik and Rus Mahommed, right at the bottom of the Gulf of Aqaba, that these handsome creatures became my diving companions.

Shuka led the way with Yoske, and Harvey and I followed a little behind. Maintaining an average depth of about twenty-five feet, we progressed through a sculptured coral shelf, accompanied by groups of inquisitive fish, including a wide-eyed Grouper, who joined us in all our subsequent dives and whom we named Oscar. The shelf on the west shore faded into a sandy slope, gradually dropping to a depth of about ninety feet before rising to the mainland beach. As we neared the northern tip of the island, we entered a forest of coral containing every imaginable species, and I photographed Harvey against a background of a fan coral so large that he appeared as a fly trapped in a gigantic web. We rose to near the surface as we reached the northern tip of the island, and then turned eastward to commence our swim south. As we turned, it was as though we had stepped out from the protection of a solid building into a blizzard; for the sea, which had shortly before been as calm as a pond, now suddenly tossed us about as the waves rushed and recoiled against the shore. We quickly dived down again to deeper water in order to avoid being crushed against the coral, and then we continued our swim southwards. Every so often Shuka, who was leading the dive, surfaced to check his position, and as he rejoined us he indicated that the sea on top remained rough.

In contrast to the west shore, the underwater terrain on the east side was more dramatic. On the west the coral reef had graduated to a gentle sand slope, whereas here the coral shelf dropped precipitously to a narrow plateau forty feet down, then there was a further drop to a yet deeper shelf at about one hundred feet, and then down into the deep blue of seeming infinity. We dived for just a minute down to the hundred-foot shelf and reflected that beneath us the sea extended to a depth of over three thousand feet, and further south in the middle of the Gulf, to something like six thousand feet. The Gulf of Aqaba is part of the great Syrian/African Rift Valley, that extraordinary split in the

47

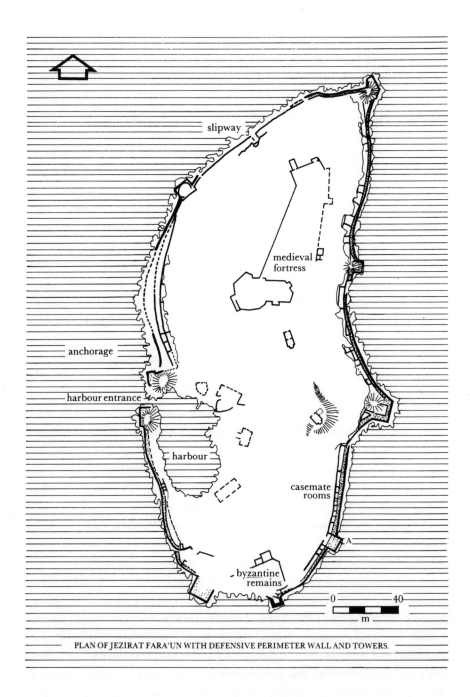

slipway

medieval
fortress

anchorage

harbour entrance

harbour

casemate
rooms

A

byzantine
remains

0 —————— 40

m

PLAN OF JEZIRAT FARA'UN WITH DEFENSIVE PERIMETER WALL AND TOWERS.

Earth's surface within which is contained the Dead Sea; the lowest spot on Earth. We continued finning southwards, keeping more or less abreast so as to cover a wide lane, and when we reached the southern tip of the island we turned westwards back into the channel, and then continued north to where we had started off. What struck us was that as soon as we turned into the channel the sea subsided just as dramatically as it had become turbulent at the northern end. Here the sea was smooth and warm and, hugging the sand slope which was peppered with small lumps of coral, we continued towards our original point of entry. It had taken us about fifty-five minutes to complete our circuit, and a little tired but content, we waded ashore and for the next hour lunched and refreshed ourselves. I reflected on the phenomenon that we had just experienced; the calm of the sea between the island and the mainland, in relation to the comparative turbulence of the open sea to the east. In retrospect, I realise that this one short experience was to affect all my future thinking about the island, but this is something on which I shall write later.

After lunch, Elisha and I took ourselves off to explore the island itself, and, clambering up the south hill, we took the path between a natural rock and loose, fallen masonry, and reached the platform at the top beside the ruins of a small building. Turning to look back on the way that we had come, I found that the view was even lovelier than I had expected, for here the broken, sepia walls of the mediaeval castle, highlighted by deep shadows on the steep hill, stood sharp against the hot blue sky, and below in the hollow between the two hills, there nestled a basin of water, its perimeter ringed by wet sand. Separating this basin from the sea, was a thin bar just a few yards wide, composed entirely of the foundations of a wall which terminated in the remains of a tower beside a thin channel connecting the sea to the basin.

In viewing the island from the top of the south hill, I had the benefit of a short account that Benno Rothenberg, the Israeli archaeologist, had given of his visit to the island in 1957. This was in his book *God's Wilderness*, and it was accompanied by a plan prepared by one of Rothenberg's colleagues, Avia Hashimshoni, an architect. In their account they described the remains of a substantial wall encircling the whole of the island, and it was this wall that I dearly wanted to examine

49

in detail. From the top of the southern hill I could see the dark borders of the wall as it extended both along the east and the west shorelines. Elisha and I descended and walked along the wall which was studded with a series of towers jutting out into the sea and the structure contained a number of architectural details which aroused my interest. There was no time now, but I was determined that I would survey this wall precisely.

The bar separating the basin or pool from the sea was an integral part of this perimeter wall. As I looked at this section closely, various details became much clearer. For example, the narrow channel which linked the pool to the sea was obviously man-made, and on each side of this channel there were the foundations of two towers. Further in around the edge of the pool, I kicked away the wet sand to reveal the top edge of a narrow wall forming a lining to the pool, and I now realised that, far from being a small, natural pool of water, what we had here was a man-made basin, an artificially constructed enclosure – a small harbour.

Some years later I came across an account given by the archaeologist Sir Leonard Woolley who, together with T E Lawrence, later to become Lawrence of Arabia, visited the island in 1913. Woolley referred to this harbour as 'a little pool of salt water'. Oh, Sir Leonard, how wrong you had been! Elisha and I could hardly contain our excitement, for it was now becoming apparent to us that the island of Jezirat Fara'un contained many mysteries to be unravelled. Rothenberg had already pointed out that the foundations of the perimeter wall were substantially earlier than those of the mediaeval castle on top of the northern hill, and that the small building surmounting the southern hill was very likely Byzantine and thus some six hundred years earlier than the mediaeval castle.

Strange as it might seem, Jezirat Fara'un was, in marine archaeological terms, virgin territory. The walls surrounding the island and its harbour were structures of enormous maritime importance, and yet they had never really attracted the interest of travellers and scholars and no attempt had ever been made to record them. Elisha and I, there and then, decided that if it was at all possible, we would correct this omission. Elisha's only regret was that he was due to leave later that year for two years' study in the United States to prepare his PhD Thesis. However, this first impression that I had of the island remained with me, and a line of research was already beginning to shape itself in my mind.

Our discussion was soon interrupted by a call from Harvey down by the water's edge. 'Come quickly,' he called, 'Shuka says he thinks he has found something.' Elisha turned to me adding, 'If Shuka says he has found something, then it's important. Let's go.' We slithered down the hillside to where Shuka was standing in the shallows. 'Get your aqualungs on quickly and come with me,' he called. Within a few minutes we had swum out to the position where he was treading water. We followed him down to a depth of about twenty feet to where he was now crouching over a small coral head. We knelt beside him and he pointed towards the underside of the coral, where he revealed the unmistakable lip of a jar. Harvey looked at me and gave me the diver's OK signal as we watched Shuka gently clearing the sand away from around the rim. In a few minutes the whole side of a fine pottery vessel became fully revealed.

I have been lucky enough to have known this moment of discovery many times, yet each new find is as thrilling as the first. Land archaeologists, as well as the underwater breed, experience that exquisite moment when an article, that has been buried for hundreds, even possibly thousands, of years, is unearthed and there is the knowledge that the last man who handled it had lived way back in the depths of history. I glanced for a moment at the others and all was silent and still except for the muffled whistles of our demand valves and the air bubbles that rose intermittently from the head of each diver.

We were anxious that Shuka should not break the vessel, but we need not have worried, for he had done this many times before. As gently as though he were holding a newly born baby, he lifted the pot from the hollow and held it up for all of us to see and we were proud indeed. It was only a practical looking pitcher but as far as we were concerned it was our first underwater find in this area and an article of treasure. We knew from experience that where one piece of pottery existed, others were likely to be found, and we spread out to search the immediate area. By the end of the dive we had located five more pieces.

51

Fortunately, these were all quite close to one another, so I was able to prepare a quick but accurate survey, and with my pocket compass, pinpointed the area by bearings taken on to the island and the mainland. On the following day we returned to lift our pieces, which we subsequently identified as Late Roman/Byzantine, and these can now be seen in the collection of pottery at the Underwater Observatory at Eilat.

During our return journey to the kibbutz, Elisha and I discussed plans for the future. His were to be with his family at Brandise University in Boston and I would arrange a joint Anglo/Israel expedition for the following year to carry out an extensive underwater survey of the sea bed around the island and to investigate further the shoreline architecture. During a short trip to Jerusalem with Harvey, I obtained authority from Dr Biran, the Director of the Department of Antiquities, and I returned home full of ideas for the organization of our expedition, and with the immediate intention of learning everything I could about the island from the pens of historians and earlier travellers.

In common with the whole of the Middle East, exploration of the Sinai blossomed at the beginning of the 19th century. Among the very first of those who visited the island was Edward Rupell, the German explorer, in 1829. He called the island Emrag, and wrote that it had been occupied by Die Emradi, a tribe he thought to be of Jewish origin. Leon de Labord, the French explorer, described how in 1836 he planted a flag on the island and 'took possession of it in the name of France'. In 1838, Lieutenant J B Wellstead of the Royal Indian Navy, sailed to the island, and he wrote a fascinating account in which he made much of the shelter afforded by the isthmus between the island and the mainland. This particular feature was also commented upon by Sir Richard Burton later in the century, and Captain Hornby, who prepared the British Admiralty Charts in 1906.

In this century C T Curelly, a colleague of the archaeologist Flinders Petrie, wrote about meeting native pearl divers working from the island, and then we get the first, albeit clumsy, attempt at a scholarly appraisal by the French traveller M R Savignac, who published some interesting photographs and an extremely inaccurate plan. I have already mentioned Woolley and Lawrence in 1913, and then after that the island appears to have been neglected until the twenties and the early thirties. Of that period I came across two particularly attractive writers: one was Major C J Jarvis, the Governor of Sinai who wrote with great love of the place. And finally there was a fascinating lady, Madame Charles Jullien, otherwise Joan Meredyth Chicherley Browden, who travelled from Egypt to Transjordan accompanied by two Bedouin. She was persuaded that a crossing to the island would be hazardous because of sharks, scorpions and jinn – ghosts. A pity! But I do like her description of the island viewed from the shore. 'The whole effect is one of great substance and harmony and at a little distance the island appears as one lengthy castle rising sharply out of the sea. The narrow windows and crumbling towers lend detail to a scene as beautiful as it is unexpected; as I stopped to watch I was somehow reminded of a placid old brown dog asleep on a blue carpet in the drowsy warmth of the afternoon sun.' I think I would rather like to have known Madame Jullien.

I had read and absorbed absolutely everything that I could find out about the island and now I longed to return to it. My plans for the expedition had gone well and I had been able to assemble a group of experienced people who were prepared to spend three weeks on the project. First there was Dick Harris, one of the most experienced divers in the British Sub-Aqua Club, who was to be my diving officer. Jerry Munday, a professional underwater cameraman, was our photographer; there was Brian Lansdown, another BS-AC diver, and Edward Goldwyn a TV producer who wanted to make a short film as part of his series on diving, and his wife Chum, our expedition doctor.

This team rendezvoused with the Israeli Group at Willi Halpert's diving centre at Eilat which was to be our expedition base. Shuka and Yoske were back again with us and they brought with them two other divers, Donny and Oded. Two of Willi's helpers, Hans from Holland and David, an Israeli, both superb divers, rounded off our team. Our first day was spent at the diving centre training the group in the search methods that I wanted to use, and preparing our equipment; and then at dawn the following day we set off on our ten-mile drive down to the island. For me it was wonderful to return; it was as if Madame Jullien's placid old brown dog was welcoming me back home.

Our underwater work continued day after day as we systematically swept the ocean bed, investigating its character and carefully locating and then plotting each and every find. Although our search was restricted to visual methods, I had brought with me from home a new instrument with which I was to experiment. This was an underwater metal detector which had been developed by Dr E T Hall of the Oxford University Laboratory of Archaeological Research. It worked on the same principle as a land metal detector and was designed to detect any metal which might lie beneath the sea bed. The instrument operated both visually and audibly, in that it had a dial and also emitted through earphones a high-pitched oscillating signal. I have good reason to recall the first occasion I put this to use. I was accompanied by Jerry Munday who, among other things, was going to take a few photographs of me using the detector. As I pushed the large instrument in front of me just above the sea bed, I became so intent on watching the dial and listening to the audio sigal, that I became quite oblivious to anything else. I suppose that I had been working on the detector for about twenty minutes or so, when something made me look up. Jerry was nowhere to be seen. Instead, about ten feet in front of me was a solid wall of barracuda. There were hundreds of them and they had formed a glistening metallic grille. The grille slowly revolved and then I realised that the fish were not swimming past me but around me; I turned one way, then the other and they were everywhere and I appeared to be the subject of their curiosity. It was a quite exquisite picture – a vast ring formed of glistening silver elements on a luminous green background. I was in a dilemma and was not sure whether to stay and absorb this once-in-a-lifetime experience, or to get the hell out of it quickly! The eyes of every single barracuda seemed to be trained on me and I was aware of the exceptionally sharp teeth of some of the larger specimens.

I was jolted into action by a momentary glimpse of Jerry's bright yellow camera beyond the circle of fish and discretion prevailed. I pushed off from the bottom and, with the detector in front of me, rammed into and through the wall of fish and then, with a few hefty kicks, I reached Jerry who had filmed the entire episode and seemed to be enjoying himself hugely. I turned and looked back to where I had been a moment before, to see the wall of barracuda as a gently undulating silver ribbon disappearing into the haze.

When we had surfaced I remonstrated with Jerry and asked him why he had not let me know that the barracuda were about. 'What?' he replied. 'And miss a marvellous shot like that?'

Later that evening all of us discussed this episode and none could recall ever having been singled out by a group of fish in this manner, let alone being encircled. We concluded that it was not I in whom the barracuda were particularly interested, but that they had been attracted by the high-pitched oscillations from the detector. I reflected that if fish in general are attracted by electronic sound, then thank heavens there were no sharks in the area.

The results of our underwater search were rewarding in that they contributed particularly to the picture that I was beginning to form of the island and of its role in history. First of all, we found that there was a great deal more material from the area in which we had located the pottery during the previous year's visit. Indeed, this turned out to be a large concentration spread over an area of about a hundred square yards, and it was all of the same period – late Roman or Byzantine. From my Mediterranean experience, I had learnt that where there were concentrations of pottery, there one might find a sunken ship. But, search as we may, there was no sign whatsoever of a wreck. At least, that is what we thought at the time, though a few years later Dr Harold Edgerton carried out a sub-sonic survey in the area that we had been examining, and his instruments revealed some thirty to forty feet beneath the sea bed, a dark shadow which, according to the Professor's interpretation, could well be a ship. Alas, this is likely to be one of those archaeological mysteries which remains unsolved solely because of the technical difficulties and expense of excavating into running sand to this depth in the sea bed.

Our collection of pottery is the largest single concentration of Byzantine material yet found in the Gulf of Aqaba, but this discovery in itself raises an interesting question. We know that the island was occupied extensively during the Crusader period because the citadel on top of the island dates from that time. We also know from historical records that a great deal of maritime activity took place during the Crusader period. Yet we found very little pottery of that period in the sea.

This puzzled me until I came across a deceptively simple explanation. The explorer Curelly, in 1906, wrote about the native pearl divers whom he had met on the island, and who he said were constantly engaged in scavenging the sea bed. 'The boat was full of odds and ends from seashells, a big turtle shell, a half dried fish, a dugong's skin stretched out to dry and scores of other things that they had found on the coral reefs. They do a little diving for pearls and informed me that they could dive to a depth of ten fathoms (sixty feet). They have a sea telescope and while searching the bottom use the canoe which they punt with great skill.' It would seem that these native divers had in fact removed absolutely everything of interest that lay on the sea bed in the early part of this century. It is significant that when we found pottery it was either hidden within clumps of coral or just beneath the sand.

I had not reckoned with the native divers, although I do recall Lieutenant Wellstead's account which he wrote some seventy years before Curelly. His Arab pilot, Surur, could, we are told, dive regularly to twenty-five fathoms – one hundred and fifty feet – and this was free diving without an aqualung

Our Byzantine pottery was an interesting discovery and reflected a period during which the island was in occupation and which could be related to the Byzantine structures on the top of the south hill; but by now my main interest was in the island itself and in particular the perimeter wall and enclosed pool which I was now certain had been a small harbour. My curiosity was spurred by our discovery of a mound of collapsed masonry near to the harbour entrance. Standing quite separate, and without any link to any structure on the island, this collapsed stone in the sea corresponded to what might have been a free-standing 'Dolphin'. This is a small tower, usually of stone or concrete, which one often sees placed near to the entrance of a harbour, and is used by craft to enable them to be man-handled into the entrance in difficult sea conditions.

Another discovery related directly to the harbour, came about quite

accidentally. We were coming to the end of our expedition and had only
one more day to go. We were on the mainland beach facing the island
loading our gear on to our vehicle. As I bent down to pick up my
aqualung, I let out a yelp. Chum came running up to me thinking, as
she explained to me later, that I had slipped a disc. But my cry was not
one of pain. On the contrary it was of delight and surprise for, at my feet
and just peeking out of the sand, I had noticed the outline of two stone
blocks. Brushing the surface sand away, the two of us revealed further
blocks running down towards the water's edge. I grabbed my mask,
dashed into the sea keeping my eyes on the line of blocks, and found
that there were more continuing in a straight line just a few inches
below the surface. These went on one after the other and finally when
they stopped I found that I was standing waist deep and some forty to
fifty-feet from the shore. What I had discovered was a jetty some twenty

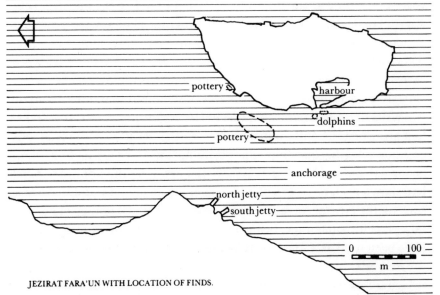

JEZIRAT FARA'UN WITH LOCATION OF FINDS.

feet wide by forty-five feet long. A great deal of the stonework was
missing but there was sufficient left to make out the general shape. This
jetty on the mainland shore was directly opposite the harbour on the
island and it was clearly intended to serve as a landing stage for a ferry.

But there was a further surprise to come after we had left the island.
I had asked Jerry Munday, who had remained behind, if he would take

some additional photographs from the top of the cliff which rose behind the main shore, and I suggested that he might also take some photographs of a rocky spur which jutted out to the sea just some fifty feet or so further north. When his photographs arrived, the shots that he had taken of the spur revealed the unmistakable linear character of a man-made structure. Strangely, when I had examined this area on the spot I had not suspected this, and yet the photograph was unmistakable. I was then reminded of a comment which Woolley made on his visit to the island. Remarking on the remains of the wall on the island he had this to say. 'The Aqaba water seems to have a curious effect of petrification (perhaps due to the coral there). It cements the shores into a single slab of conglomerate; this wall therefore looks as natural a tip stratum as need be save for the toolmarks still showing in the inner edge of some stones.' What Woolley was saying was that the effect of the sea very soon changed the appearance of man-made masonry into what appears to be natural stone. Jerry's photographs had revealed a second structure on the mainland shore, and in my view this is almost certainly the remains of a landing stage, and by the size of the stonework, corresponds very closely to the masonry of the island wall.

Arriving back in England I was able to sit quietly and think about the two visits that I had made to the island. Over the previous three weeks I had absorbed the environment and seen the sea in its various moods, and one nagging question kept cropping up. Here we had an island facing a mainland between which was a narrow isthmus of water which had shown itself to be a sheltered anchorage; in fact, it was described as such by the official Naval Sailing Charts as 'The anchorage of Fara'un Island'. This anchorage, being a natural phenomenon, would certainly have been used as a safe haven by sailors for as long as men have sailed the Red Sea.

Combined with this anchorage, we had a small enclosed harbour on the island, and both the island and the harbour were encircled by the remains of a massive defensive wall. I came to the conclusion that the harbour would at one time have been a natural inlet, but had been formed into an artificial harbour by the building of a bar separating the bay from the isthmus, and the defensive wall had then been continued over this bar.

It now seemed quite clear that what I had here was a maritime installation not only of substantial size but also of considerable complexity and subtlety. How was it, therefore, that the naval and maritime significance of this place had hardly been touched upon by previous travellers and archaeologists? True, some had remarked on the safety of the anchorage, but the archaeologists in particular had either totally missed, or disregarded it.

I suppose that the answer must be that archaeologists as a group have taken very little interest in shoreline buildings, and have thought little in maritime terms. Their disinterest in the shore is presumably because scientific archaeology is based on stratigraphy and the ability to dig into the ground so as to reveal stratigraphic layers which can be studied at leisure and in a systematic manner. In general this is not possible on the shoreline, for as any child who builds sand castles will know, the sea has little respect for man-made structures. Thus we see that coastal structures and buildings and the shoreline have been more or less ignored by the land archaeologist, and it is only in recent years that the new breed of maritime archaeologist has begun to work in these areas.

As I sorted through my notes and drawings in preparation for the paper that I was writing, I began to realise that my conclusions would be incomplete without a detailed survey of the perimeter wall. Mindful, however, of the other underwater projects to which I was committed, I set myself a programme over the next few years of tagging on two or three days at the end of each of my visits to Israel in order to go down to the Red Sea to continue with the survey of the wall.

Mapping the wall was a slow process, for all that was left of the structure was mainly the stone blocks that remained flush with the ground or a few inches above sea level. These foundations were 'in general' indistinct and their visibility depended a lot on the light and angle of the sun. One day I would finish off my survey on a particular spot, and the next day I would have difficulty in locating where I had left off. With experience, however, I gradually accustomed my eyes to the general patterning of the wall and worked my way around inch by inch.

The towers were easier to distinguish, as in many cases the base courses were intact and clear, particularly where the towers projected into the sea. This gave me the recipe for surveying the rest of the wall when I realised that the stones became much clearer after wetting. The natural ground or rubble tended to absorb the water more rapidly, whereas the building blocks dried off a little more slowly. The wall encircled the island completely. There were eight, or possibly nine, towers of which two flanked the entrance to the harbour. I found a slipway that perforated the wall opposite the mainland, and at the southern end there appeared to be a sea gate. The outside part of the wall is of composite construction, comprising of an outer skin of large cyclopic blocks averaging about three feet thick with an inner skin half

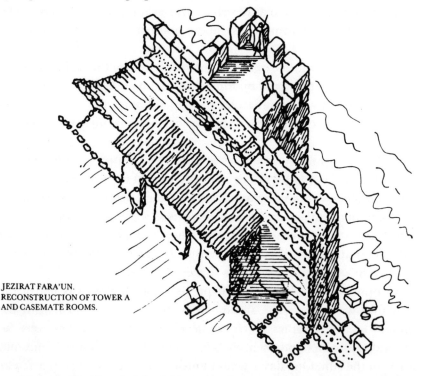

JEZIRAT FARA'UN.
RECONSTRUCTION OF TOWER A
AND CASEMATE ROOMS.

as thick again. Sandwiched between these two skins is seven feet of compressed rubble, so that the total thickness of the outer wall alone is about twelve feet. Built against the inside face of this wall there were casemate rooms some seven feet deep which would have been the living accommodation for those who manned the walls.

The time came when I had finally completed my survey of the wall and the harbour, and what conclusions had I come to? I had now become thoroughly familiar with this setting; Jezirat Fara'un, a small island separated from the Sinai shore by a narrow sheltered anchorage, and on the island a man-built enclosed harbour and the island itself surrounded by a defensive wall. This combination of natural and man-made features had a familiar ring, and I was struck by the very close resemblance of this complex to the Phoenician harbours in the Mediterranean. The harbours of Sidon, Tyre and Arwad in the Phoenician homeland all comprise small harbours on offshore islands, and this pattern is also repeated in the western Mediterranean on the island of Motya on the west coast of Sicily which was colonised by the Phoenicians.

The resemblance between Jezirat Fara'un and the Mediterranean examples is so close that one is immediately prompted to ask whether the Phoenicians ever ventured into the Red Sea? The answer to this question is that they most certainly did, and the manner in which they had cause to come here is told in the Bible in Kings 9, the passage I have used to begin this chapter. It tells of the commercial enterprise entered into between King Solomon and King Hiram of Tyre, and of the maritime trade enterprise developed jointly by these two rulers. Solomon realised that his country's access to the Red Sea gave him the potential of unlimited trade with Africa and the East. But his sailors' experience was limited to short range coastal sailing and Solomon was wise enough to appreciate that he needed the navigational skills of the Phoenicians. This was to be the second of the two Kings' joint enterprises, for Hiram had already provided the skilled craftsmen for the building of King Solomon's Temple.

One can quite imagine what Hiram's first reaction might have been to Solomon's proposal. An operation of this sort would need a good port and it is unlikely that the King would have embarked on an enterprise of this magnitude without first seeking the advice of his advisors. In a flight of fancy, this is the sort of report which I imagine Hiram's chief mariner would have sent back to his King.

'Sir, I arrived in Eloth a few days ago and have been busily engaged in carrying out a reconnaissance of the seashore with the object of finding a suitable location for your harbour for, as you will understand, a fleet without a safe shelter is doomed. I had hoped that I might find a suitable site close to King Solomon's city Eloth, but having walked far along the shore both to the west and to the east, I have found nothing but sand and shingle beaches, and at no place is there a part of the sea which is protected from the storms which arise very quickly in these parts. The servants of King Solomon, however, have told me of an island which is called Ezion Geber, and they say that their fathers recall stories of ships of the Pharaohs being anchored here many years in the past. I went therefore to Ezion Geber, where I had been told that there is a channelled sea between the island and the mainland which remains calm when the sea elsewhere is turbulent. Indeed, I found this to be true and I am satisfied that this is the best haven in the region. The journey from Eloth took us two-and-a-half hours and on the way we passed a place where there were many trees and water wells. I recommend therefore that this island can be built upon so that it can be made into a very suitable port. As you know, we have in our homeland and in the great sea to the west, very similar anchorages, and it is our custom to build a small protected harbour on the island so that in severe emergencies the most important vessels may be brought in from the anchorage. The harbour will also provide a means of unloading conveniently. At Ezion Geber it will not be difficult to provide such a harbour, for in this case there exists on the island a small bay facing the mainland. The sea here is shallow and we can easily separate the bay from the anchorage by building a mole across the open end of the bay. We shall leave a narrow entrance into the harbour, and on this mole we shall build a wall which we will then continue right around the whole of the island. Within this wall we will build a series of towers in strategic positions, similar to the walled towns with which Your Majesty and King Solomon are already familiar, having built many of these in your lands. But it will not be necessary for your boats to be built here, for they can be built at Eloth which is better for the housing of your artificers. The boats will be launched at

Eloth and sailed to Ezion Geber, where they will be moored
in safety. I also recommend that the road from the city Eloth
to its harbour be cleared of rock and obstruction, for there
will be much traffic here. Opposite the island we will build
such moles as are necessary so that goods and men can be
conveyed conveniently to and from the island. This island of
Ezion Geber is the place where you must harbour your fleet,
for there is no other place.'

My conclusions had finally brought me to the certainty that Jezirat
Fara'un is the site of Ezion Geber, the port of the ancient city of
Eloth, and my flight of fancy is as good a way as any of giving my
reasons. But I would also like to present some further evidence in
support of this contention. I referred to the Egyptian Pharaohs
having used this site at an earlier date, and this is based on Rothenberg's evidence of pottery which he collected on the island. He
identified this pottery with the period of the Midianites, which is
similar to the pottery found at his excavations at Timna, the site of the
Egyptian Hator Temple of the 12th and 13th centuries BC. Rothenberg
relates his temple to the copper-mining industries in the Negev Desert
of the Late Bronze/Early Iron Age Period corresponding to the
Rameses Pharaohs. This had led Rothenberg to suggest that the island
of Jezirat Fara'un was originally a mining harbour used by the
Egyptians and, in support of this, he points out the remains of a small
metallurgical installation on the island, evidence of small-scale iron-
smelting activity.

In geographical and in maritime terms, the case for our island being
Ezion Geber is, I maintain, convincingly argued, but if I were to turn
devil's advocate against myself, I would query whether the architectural character of the vast perimeter casemate wall can positively be
identified with the Solomonic Period. The Phoenician marine walls in
the Mediterranean with which I am familiar, do not bear a great
resemblance to our perimeter wall, and it is for this reason that I am
inclined to agree with the local interpretation, that these walls are in
fact of the Byzantine period, particularly in view of the fact that the
small harbour is surrounded by remains which are certainly Byzantine.
But this contention hardly dents my argument. I will explain why.

There is ample evidence that the Crusader castle atop the hills of the island was built from the stones of the perimeter wall which they had demolished. If one looks closely at the round tower on the island facing west, it will be seen that the base comprises large cyclopic blocks similar to the rest of the wall, whereas the upper part is of the mediaeval period resembling exactly that of the castle. By the same token, therefore, I suggest that the original Solomonic marine structure would have been dismantled by the Byzantines for them to build their wall thereon.

From the reader who is familiar with biblical archaeology I would expect to hear: 'What about Nelson Glueck and the site of Tell el-Kheleifeh?' This is a story which I will relate because it refers to a previous identification of the site of Ezion Geber, an identification which had already been discredited before I came on the scene. It is, in my view, a rather sad and emotive story, and deals with the work of Nelson Glueck, the eminent American theological scholar and archaeologist. Glueck, who had spent a lifetime exploring and excavating the Negev Desert, came upon the site of Tell el-Kheleifeh, an ancient mound just west of Aqaba, and having produced evidence of copper-smelting and Iron Age pottery, proclaimed this as the site of Ezion Geber/Eloth. This was in 1939 and the scholarly world accepted this interpretation and every authoritative book quoted it for the next quarter of a century. In the early 1950s, Benno Rothenberg, who had been Glueck's photographer, mounted his own expeditions into the Negev, and in particular the Valley of Timna, and concluded that Glueck's evidence was tenuous and suspect. The archaeological establishment did not take kindly to this attack on Glueck's reputation, but Rothenberg and others relentlessly pursued their quarry, and in 1965 Glueck, by then aged and revered, published the following disclaimer.

> 'We find ourselves compelled . . . and in the view of new knowledge and some continuing criticisms of our initial reports, to revise radically some of our original conclusions. The location of the Tell in the middle of the southern end of the Wadi Arabah, its possession of the first potable water however brackish as one comes from the western side of the

(above) *Examples of over 300 terracotta votive figurines of the Phoenician Goddess Tanit recovered from the wreck site at Shave Zion.*

(left) *An enlargement of the Sign of Tanit with the outline of a swathed child at the top offered as sacrifice to the Goddess.*

The island of Jezirat Fara'un (Coral Island) in the Gulf of Aqaba, the probable site of King Solomon's Harbour of Ezion Geber described in the Bible in Kings 9.

Jezirat Fara'un from the air. The small enclosed harbour and the natural anchorage between the island and the mainland are clearly seen.

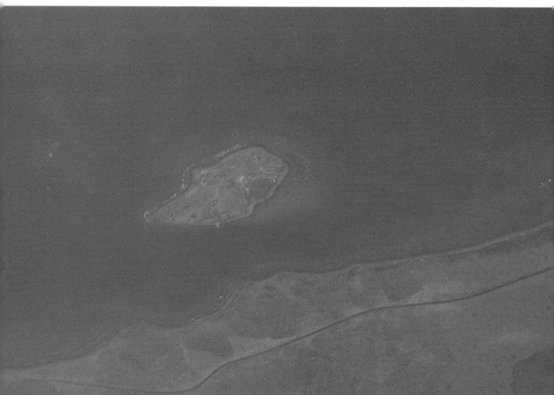

The David Roberts lithograph of Jezirat Fara'un which he called the Island of Graia and which he visited in 1839. The artist has drawn himself in the foreground.

The small enclosed harbour at Jezirat Fara'un approached through the narrow entrance from the sheltered anchorage.

The remains of one of the two quays which we found on the mainland shore directly opposite the island.

The City of Acre; surely one of the most evocative maritime views in the Middle East.

We used an air-lift to clear the sand from the wreck of one of Napoleon's ships which Sydney Smith sank as a block-ship in the entrance to the harbour in his defence of Acre in 1799.

The ruined Tower of Flies which guarded the entrance to the harbour at Acre. It figured prominently in the Crusader wars and was finally destroyed in the naval bombardment by Admiral Stopford in 1840.

(above) *The Crusaders at Caesarea built this quay from pillars taken from the Herodian city built eleven centuries earlier.*

(right) *One of the Greek Fire grenades found at Acre. Greek Fire was the deadly napalm of the medieval Orient and was used by both the Moslims and Crusaders in their battles for Acre.*

(overleaf) *The imprint of the now submerged Herodian harbour of Sebastos at Caesarea is seen stretching out to sea in this aerial photograph. Its entrance is top right beside the boat of Edwin Link who carried out the first undersea investigation of the harbour remains in 1960.*

The Roman aquaduct which brought freshwater from a spring five miles north of King Herod's maritime City of Caesarea.

The medieval builders of the Crusader City at Caesarea used the granite columns of Herod's City to reinforce their walls.

(above) *Emulating his Roman patrons, Herod built a* piscina *(fish-tank) at Caesarea. The mosaic terrace that we discovered with remains of columns and capitols are evidence of the luxurious architecture of the* piscina.

(right) *This syphon bored into the rock is activated by wave action and provides the motive force for extracting the water from the* piscina *and thus stimulating the water's circulation.*

Moments after the discovery of the mosaic terrace beside the piscina, *Trudie Flinder carefully brushes the sand from its surface.*

Sluice gates were inserted into the channels in both the piscinas at Caesarea and Lapithos for the careful control of water flow. The grooves into which the sluice gates were slotted can clearly be seen.

The wreck of the 18th-century merchant ship in the Red Sea contained a cargo of hundreds of small earthenware decorated pots. The position of the pottery is carefully mapped by divers before removal and in the background there can be seen scaffolding over the wreck used for stereoscopic photography.

The hull of the wreck is carefully surveyed by the divers.

The three small bronze figurines of Roman Gods found in the sea at Shikmona by thirteen-year-old Udi Galilee.

The author and a colleague using the underwater metal detector in the Red Sea.

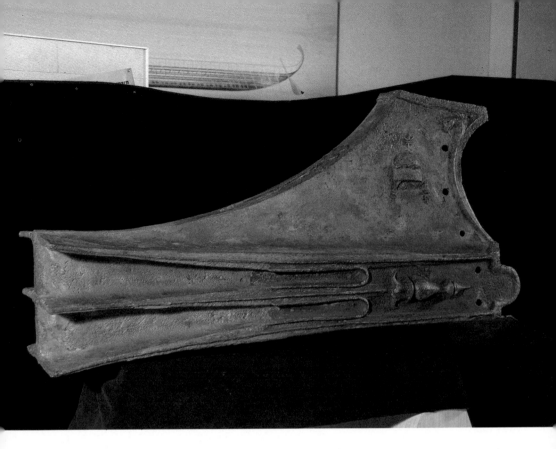

This is the only bronze ram from an ancient warship that has ever been found. 'The ballistic missile of the ancient world,' said Professor Richard Steffy – 'this ram is impressive, almost hypnotic at first glance. I had not expected so much beauty, technology and expertise to be lavished on an ancient warship.'

north shore of the Gulf, and the fact that the shoreline in front of it is free from rocks, and that small boats could have been drawn up on it or anchored close to it, add up to the sum of its natural advantages. The site, however, is easily bypassed. Its position is not a commanding one.'

Professor Glueck's disclaimer came as a considerable shock to Middle East archaeologists who had hung on his words for three decades. The editor of *The Biblical Archaeologist* in whose pages Glueck's report appeared in 1956, observed, 'Glueck's new ideas on the matter are extremely important, as they demonstrate a capacity to change cherished convictions gracefully.' This sad little episode, however, has confirmed to me that ancient maritime sites cannot be assessed solely on traditional archaeological criteria. One of Glueck's lifelong ambitions had been to identify the site of Ezion Geber but, although he had personally visited Jezirat Fara'un some years earlier, he was entirely incapable of recognising the island's maritime installations. Harbour, anchorages, quays, meant nothing to him and he failed to understand them on Jezirat Fara'un. Woolley and Lawrence were no different, for to them the harbour was 'a little pool of water'. Nowadays, when many land archaeologists are acknowledging the potential of maritime archaeology, such errors are fortunately more rare.

I cannot finish this chapter without reference to an intriguing theory which came to me via Elisha Linder. Elisha's Professor at Brandise University was the eminent Middle East scholar Cyrus H Gordon. Professor Gordon, who had played a leading part in the deciphering of the Cretan Linear-A Text, had long worked on the theory that the sailors of the ancient Middle East, and particularly the Phoenicians, had reached the South Americas, and that there was an intimate cultural connection between Pre-Columbian Messo-Americans and the Phoenicians. Indeed, in recent years this theory has been reinforced, particularly by the explorer Thor Heyerdahl. Dr Gordon's support for this theory is based on his study of ancient Pre-Columbian texts from various parts of America. In 1967 a copy of one of these texts was brought to him, and although there is a formidable body of scholarly opinion that this text is a fake, Gordon is entirely convinced that it is not only genuine, but that this text, known as the Paraiba Text, is of Canaanite/Hebrew origin. This is its translation:

> 'We are Sons of Canaan from Sidon, the City of the Kings. Commerce has cast us on this distant shore, a land of mountains. We offered a youth to the exalted gods and goddesses in the nineteenth year of Hiram our Mighty King. We embarked from Ezion Geber into the Red Sea and voyaged with ten ships. We were at sea together for two years around Africa but were separated by a storm and were no longer with our companions. So we came here twelve men and three women on a new shore which I, the Admiral, will control. Verily may the exalted gods and goddesses favour us well.'

I have no doubt that Professor Gordon's theory will for many years be supported by some with enthusiasm, and opposed by many others with scorn. For my part, I return as often as I can to this beautiful small island in the Red Sea to indulge myself in the pleasure of sitting on its shore and imbibing the vibrations of history that emanate from its stones.

V

Napoleon, Smith and Jezzah the Butcher

Yonder is the key to the East.

NAPOLEON'S CHIEF OF STAFF BEFORE ACRE, 1799

I suppose if anyone were to ask me what is my favourite Middle East city, Acre might come near to the top of the list. There are many reasons to account for my affection for this place. There is, of course, its maritime history going back thousands of years, its melodramatic architecture, and the fact that its alleyways are still lived in and hum to the exciting bustle of people going about their everyday life. There are markets with the mingling smells of fish and spices, while beneath the mediaeval arches the boat repairer still wields his adze, and the copper craftsman hammers the most intricate of patterns.

'Elisha and I will be joint directors of a British/Israeli underwater archaeological expedition to Acre later this year; how about coming out and joining us?' My proposal was put in the course of conversation to

Professor E T Hall after I heard the paper he had given on the subject of the use of electronic instruments for underwater searching at a conference at the Institute of Archaeology in London. To my great delight he replied, 'What a splendid idea! Yes, of course I will.' As the Director of the Laboratory of Archaeological Research at Oxford University, Teddy Hall had developed the proton magnetometer for marine use, which he had used very successfully on the location of World War One battleships in the Turkish Dardanelles. Fortuitously, his boat, *Blue Bonito*, a high-speed launch, which was more or less a floating laboratory, was at that time berthed at Kyrenia in Cyprus, only a few hours sailing from Acre.

Later that year, Trudie and I welcomed Teddy and his wife Jeffi as they stepped on to the site of the ancient breakwater at Acre, and within a couple of days, with his assistants Dave Wallington and Phil Wigmore, he was ready to start work with the magnetometer. This instrument is designed to measure the magnetic field of the Earth and is capable of detecting metal on or under the sea bed, and even large quantities of pottery which has a magnetic content because of the hard clay from which the pottery is made. The magnetometer consisted of a small torpedo-shaped detector which was pulled on a cable behind the boat; this floated a couple of feet above the sea bed and picked up signals, which were then transmitted through to a moving pen which marked delicate traces on a revolving paper roll. When nothing was being detected, the pen produced a straight line, but immediately an anomaly was picked up it would begin to move about. It would produce varying shapes according to the nature of the anomaly, so that a cannonball would read as a long stiletto-like trace, whereas metal spread over a large area would show up as a broad pattern with jagged edges.

Elisha had been working on the ancient harbour at Acre, and the object of our joint expedition was to carry out a general underwater search of the whole harbour area and the waters leading up to this, concentrating on certain features. Teddy's task was to search the sea bed areas in a systematic manner and mark spots with buoys when anything was detected. Thereafter, we would dive in the area to see whether we could locate the anomaly.

As the days went by, Teddy and his team became more experienced in recognising the type of anomaly from the trace it had recorded. But as the instrument showed equal preference for ancient, historical, and modern material, Teddy's first interesting discovery was an attractive brass bedstead, circa 20th century. Cannonballs from the 18th and 19th centuries proliferated as did Coca Cola tins. Nevertheless, the magnetometer began to locate some interesting material, including three large 18th-century anchors.

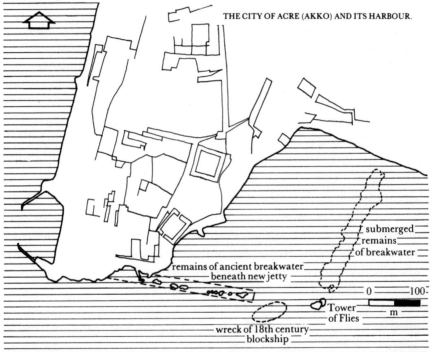

THE CITY OF ACRE (AKKO) AND ITS HARBOUR.

submerged remains of breakwater

remains of ancient breakwater beneath new jetty

0 ———— 100.
m

Tower of Flies

wreck of 18th century blockship

One day *Blue Bonito* was working the area between the end of the breakwater and a free-standing stone structure which stood out of the sea by itself. This is called the Tower of Flies, about which I will have more to say in the next chapter. When the boat passed over this spot, the magnetometer began to record small, but fairly consistent signals and, as the boat crossed and re-crossed the position, the pen repeated the same sort of trace. Teddy dropped a buoy overboard and in the evening reported to me that there was an anomaly in this area that he thought worth investigating.

Early the following day, Chaim, Shuka and I dived on the spot marked by the buoy. The depth was about twenty-five feet but we could see nothing except the sandy sea bed covered with odd bits of flotsam. After a short interval we met back at the weight which held the buoy and agreed by visual signals that we would again go off in different directions, but this time would dig into the sand with our knives and search beneath the sea bed itself. After about ten minutes or so I felt a resistance to my knife, and began to brush the sand away. And then I felt a tap on my shoulder. I turned to see Shuka beckoning me. We both swam over to where Chaim knelt on the sea bed. He pointed downwards and brushed the sand away to reveal first one plank of wood, and then next to it another; then a metal spike and another. We nodded excitedly at each other, for we knew that beneath us lay the remains of a sunken boat.

The whole of the next day was spent in clearing the sea bed with our air-lift. This is the under-water archaeologist's standard excavating tool. It consists of a plastic or metal tube about six inches in diameter. Running alongside this tube is an air-line bringing down compressed air supplied from the surface. The bottom of the air-line is then turned into the lower end of the large tube and when air is forced down from the compressor on the surface, it escapes from the hose and then rushes up the air-lift tube, expanding and accelerating rapidly as it speeds towards the surface. This has the effect of creating a powerful suction, so that anything placed in the opening of the air-lift pipe is immediately sucked up to the surface. Its use as an excavating tool is to enable the diver to wave away the sand or mud on the sea bed, with his hand or with a trowel, and then shift this waste over to the mouth of the air-lift so that it can be sucked to the surface. In this manner a skilled operator can remove layers of the sea bed inch by inch without unduly disturbing the archaeological material. If, by accident, any important material is sucked up, it is collected at the other end of the air-lift, which is near the surface, where a large basket is attached.

Fortunately for us, the site was near the end of the breakwater, so all that we had to do was to wheel the compressor to the end, rig up our pipework, and within an hour we were prepared to go. At the end of the day we had cleared an area of the sea bed some forty feet long by twenty

86

feet wide, to reveal a part of the hull of a ship consisting of planking, sheathed on the underside with copper sheeting, and a great number of copper nails and spikes still in position.

We were lucky to have with us on the expedition Peter Throckmorton, the pioneer underwater archaeologist who had himself, just a few years before, been responsible for the discovery of the oldest wreck yet found, dating to 1200 BC. Peter, a ship expert, was able to assure us, however, that this wreck was nowhere near that age, but likely to date from the 18th century, and that from its constructional characteristics, appeared to be a battleship of the Second or Third Line and probably of French origin. It was, he said, probably about a hundred and fifty feet long, with a tonnage of between eight hundred to one thousand tons.

We continued to clear as much of the site as possible and then carried out a survey of the hull. I should explain that in common with most wrecks of wooden ships, the hull had broken open and our survey was not of a whole ship but of its remains which had become flattened on the sea bed. Other than removing some of the spikes and copper for laboratory testing, we decided to leave the whole hull on the sea bed. We covered the area once again with sand so that the remains might be protected as much as possible, and then put our minds to discussing the wreck's origin.

The one thing that struck us as odd about this wreck was that other than the hull itself, we found no contents whatsoever. There were no armaments or any of the fixtures that are usually found on a boat of this sort, and even the decks were missing. Our discovery had revealed nothing other than the hull and its corresponding supporting structure. Our assumption at the time was not an unreasonable one. We deduced that as the boat had sunk in comparatively shallow water, it had been salvaged by local divers who had removed everything that was worth taking.

The discovery of our 18th-century wreck was an interesting one, but in particular it demonstrated the proton magnetometer's worth, for it is unlikely that this wreck would ever have been re-discovered without an instrument of this sort. Having returned home and written up the results of our Acre expedition, our wreck had pretty well slipped from my mind until, one day when I happened to be in the map room of the

British Museum doing some research on another site, I came across a folio entitled *Acre*. Thumbing casually through its contents I saw a small map of Acre harbour with the disposition of a large number of ships. It was titled 'Plan of the Siege of Acre. Raised May 20th 1799.' This was the siege of the city carried out by Napoleon at the very end of the 18th century and, as I examined the map closely, I realised that our wreck adjoining the Tower of Flies related closely to this action.

Let me explain briefly the story of the siege. Napoleon, who had by then occupied Egypt for some years, was determined to control Palestine as well for he realised that by this route he could reach the 'soft underbelly of Europe' and his path would then be clear to his ultimate goal, Imperial Russia. With thirty thousand troops at his command, the Emperor swept virtually unopposed up the coast of Palestine to arrive at the gates of Acre on 18th March 1799. Standing on an ancient Tell overlooking the city, General Murat, Napoleon's Chief of Staff, pointed down to the city exclaiming, 'Yonder is the key to the East.' Napoleon, anticipating some resistance from the city's ruler, Jezzah Pasha, loaded his siege guns into two flotillas of naval craft at Alexandria, and sent these ahead by sea. News of the advance had reached Jezzah Pasha who, having no stomach for a fight, was preparing to evacuate the town, when there suddenly appeared offshore His Majesty's ships *Tigre* and *Theseus*, two ships of a British squadron commanded by Captain William Sidney Smith. Smith persuaded Jezzah to remain with his Turkish troops in defence of the city, and Napoleon now faced, as he was to find to his cost, a formidable pair.

Jezzah, known as The Butcher to his subjects, had once been a Bosnian slave and had risen to his position by way of a career of intrigue, ruthlessness and savage cruelty. Smith's background was no less colourful. Born in 1764, he enlisted at the age of twelve and served in the American War of Independence. He was loaned to the King of Sweden in that country's war against Russia for which he was rewarded with a knighthood and, having been recalled to the Royal Navy after an absence of eight years for active service against the French, finally landed up in a French prison condemned for piracy. Here he stayed for two years until rescued by a French officer, Colonel Phelippeux, who thereafter accompanied Smith as his friend and military adviser. After serving under Nelson in the Mediterranean, it was decided that he would be put to best use away from the main fleet and in command of an independent marauding squadron.

At Acre, Smith immediately put Phelippeux in command of the land forces and went off to prepare for the ambush of Napoleon's siege guns, of which he had received prior intelligence. The Commander of the French Naval Squadron, which was transporting the siege guns, was unaware of what awaited him at Acre and, continuing northwards and rounding the Cape of Carmel, ran smack into the *Tigre* and the *Theseus*. Being no match for the two British men-of-war, the Frenchman turned and ran, but was soon overtaken and captured. Smith's booty consisted of seven gun vessels with thirty-four guns and two hundred and thirty-eight men. The British Commander lost no time in returning to Acre and the guns, originally intended for the destruction of Acre, were now deployed in its defence. Smith stationed the captured gun boats *La Negresse, La Foudre, La Dangereuse, La Marie Rose, La Verge de Grace, La Deux Frères* and *La Torride* close to his battleships *Tigre* and *Theseus* offshore. He placed a captured brass eighteen-pounder on the Tower of Flies and a thirty-six pounder carronade on a barge moored to the ancient mole.

The Siege of Acre went on for sixty fearful days with seldom an hour devoid of gunfire and the savagery of hand-to-hand fighting. The air was putrid with the stench of unburied corpses and, while Smith conducted a brilliant defence of the town, the Pasha sat in state dispensing awards for the mounting pile of infidel heads which surrounded him. Despite the spectacular victory of a small, well-disciplined force of French infantry against twenty-five thousand horsemen on Mount Tabor only twenty-five miles to the East of Acre, Napoleon's army was rapidly becoming demoralised; and, struck by an outbreak of plague, Napoleon was forced to raise the siege having lost eight Generals, eighty Superior Officers and four thousand men. On 20th May he withdrew and retreated back to Egypt.

After the very last assault, Sidney Smith had, in fact, informed the British Government that he feared the town could not withstand another attack. Thus for two short months the whole future history of Europe depended on whether this small maritime city in Palestine would be able to withstand the might of the greatest military commander of the age. Had Napoleon succeeded in being victorious in Acre, nothing could have stopped him from sweeping up towards Russia. As he ruefully said in later years, 'Had Acre fallen I should have changed the face of the World.' As for Sidney Smith, he was knighted by a grateful King, and the Nation dubbed him The Lion of Acre. In his later years, he retired to Paris where he died at the age of seventy-six, and was buried at Père Lachaise in an area reserved for Napoleon's Generals, in the very year that the remains of Napoleon himself were brought back to Paris from St Helena.

Let us revert to the small map that I found in the British Museum and the 18th-century battleship that we discovered at Acre. The map was prepared by one of Sidney Smith's junior officers, and is a plan showing the key positions of the defending ships during the siege. It shows a ship positioned between the end of the breakwater and the Tower of Flies, and this related exactly to the position of the wreck that we had found on the sea bed. But what mystified me was that in the legend on the plan, the ship was identified as 'a wreck filled with sand.' What did this strange phrase mean? I pondered, and then the penny dropped. Of course, the wreck filled with sand was a blockship. Smith, in his defence of the city and the harbour, had adopted the classic defence method of sinking a ship in the harbour mouth so that it would be impossible for any attacking vessel to enter. He had used one of the vessels captured from the French off Haifa, and stripped it entirely, removing its deck, sinking it in the harbour entrance and filling it with sand. This was why we had found nothing other than the hull of the ship itself. And there it has remained for any diver to swim down to and rediscover for himself.

VI

The Tower of Flies

*The end of our voyage from Tyre came when we landed at
Ptolemais where we greeted the brothers and stayed one day
with them.*

ST PAUL – THE ACTS OF THE APOSTLES 2.7

At our home in London I have a glass display cabinet in which I keep
various modest momentoes of our underwater expeditions. Amongst
those from Acre are two bronze spikes from our Napoleonic blockship,
and two pieces from a very much earlier period. The first is a small
pottery sherd from the 3rd century BC when the city was known as
Ptolemais. Then there is a small coin dating from the time of the Roman
conquest of the city over the Greeks. Acre shares with one or two other
Levant cities the distinction of a more or less continuous occupation
from the very earliest of times, and one of the tasks of our Acre
expedition was to see whether we could locate anything underwater

91

which would help us to illuminate the earlier maritime history of this ancient port.

If you stand on the quayside at Acre and look out to sea, you will see the ruined remains of a small tower which stands more or less alone at the entrance to the harbour. I have already mentioned this tower in connection with our blockship find. It surprised me to learn from Elisha that no one to date had attempted to record this structure and so I decided to correct this omission by surveying it completely, including its foundations below sea level. From historical documents, it is known that the tower was used as a lighthouse in the 18th century, and during the Crusader period it defended the entrance to the harbour and as such was one of the city's main bastions. The derivation of its name is obscure and is lost in the depths of antiquity, but there are a couple of theories that are worth recounting. The first is that this sea fort was the site of a rock on which the Canaanite god Baal was worshipped. Among his various qualities, the worshippers of Baal knew him as a god of the sea, and the Ugaritic text from the 14th century BC talks of Baal's victory over the sea god Yamm. Baal is also known in the Bible as Baal-Zebub, which translates as Lord of the Flies. There is also a story that the tower was used by the Phoenicians as a site for sacrifice, a feature of Canaanite worship, and the name Tower of Flies was supposed to come from the swarms of insects that enveloped the area after sacrificial ceremonies.

It did not take long to measure up the tower above sea level, and then we set about the task of surveying the underwater foundations. Peter Throckmorton's wife, Joan, who is an excellent draftswoman, assisted me. The first thing that I noted about the structure was that the character of the masonry below sea level differed from that above the surface. The walls above sea level were made of small blocks of dressed masonry, the style being very typical of that seen in many mediaeval castles scattered throughout the Middle East; whereas the walls below sea level presented quite a different picture. Here, instead of small blocks, we had very large blocks of stone – the term often used is Cyclopic – and these stones were laid header fashion, that is, the ends of the blocks facing outwards and their length extending into the structure. At its shallowest point, the bottom was only a few feet below the surface and in these shallow depths the detailed measuring of the foundations was a far from pleasant occupation for the surface was always liable to chop up and we were vulnerable not only to surface waves, but also to the washes from passing boats. I found that the best thing that I could do was to put three weightbelts around me and anchor myself to the bottom as solidly as possible.

Soon, however, we moved into water where the foundations were deeper, and day by day we continued with our task, measuring and tagging each block with its individual number – a slow and tedious process. At this stage we did not expect to find anything particularly spectacular, but hoped that our study of the character of the masonry, when finally put on to the drawing board, would enable us to assess the earlier periods of the tower more accurately.

But there was a surprise in store. One day we were working our way along the south face. It was approaching noon, and our air was beginning to run out. We decided to finish our morning session, so we stripped off our aqualungs and gathered our gear together to await the motor boat which would take us back to base. As it was a hot day we cooled down by snorkelling on the surface in the area of the west end of the tower near the end of the breakwater. As I floated lazily on the surface I looked down through my mask at the odd fish swimming by and at the swaying kelp which tended to predominate in this area, and as I did so my eye was momentarily attracted by what appeared to be a series of parallel, thin black lines. I pointed these out to Joan and we dived down to see what they were. The black lines turned out to be a series of deep fissures in the rock into which we could just about squeeze our hands; they were absolutely parallel and evenly spaced about a yard apart. We quickly surfaced to collect our aqualungs with the little air that each of us had in our bottles, and speedily carried out an examination of our find. To our surprise we could see that the fissures were narrow, open joints between a whole series of extremely large, well-fashioned stone foundation blocks some of which were over three feet by three feet in section and twelve feet long. This was a very substantial foundation structure indeed, for the bottom course lay at a depth of nearly twenty feet. What was even more interesting was that the course of blocks as they lay one above the other were stepped towards the end. There were seven steps in all and when we removed some of the kelp we found that the blocks were in immaculate shape and laid in a precise manner.

What was odd was that we must have swum over this position countless times before and yet we had never noticed these fissures. The blocks had been covered by long kelp and I realised that the reason we had noticed the fissures on this occasion was that we had been snorkelling at exactly the time of the day when the noon sun was in the position to penetrate the sea and cast just a sufficient amount of shadow.

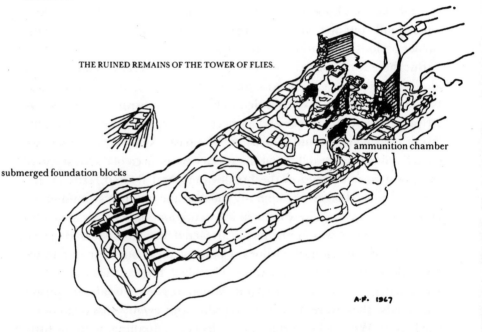

THE RUINED REMAINS OF THE TOWER OF FLIES.

ammunition chamber

submerged foundation blocks

A.P. 1967

Our survey complete, we were now able to arrive at some interim conclusions about the Tower of Flies and its structure. There is no doubt that the original foundations are very old indeed, and I would hazard a guess that these relate to the Phoenician period. I base this view on the style in which the blocks are laid which is header fashion, a characteristic of Phoenician/Canaanite Bronze Age construction. At sea level, the character of the masonry changes from that of the earlier period to that of mediaeval stonework, where the masonry is not only typically mediaeval, but we also see the use of stone blocks bonded together by iron clamps fixed with caulking lead. On the uppermost levels of the tower it is still possible to recognise the elements of the lighthouse which was built by the Turks in the 17th or 18th century, and which was finally destroyed in the naval bombardment of Acre by Admiral Stopford in 1840. Recently, I came across a splendid 18th-century naval lithograph which shows the Tower of Flies blowing up in a terrific explosion. This explosion is linked to another discovery made by three of our Israeli colleagues a couple of days after Joan and I had finished our survey.

They noticed that an area behind the south wall of the tower was composed of loose rubble stonework which had the appearance of having tumbled down from the superstructure. They set about removing these stones one by one and, so as to avoid being hampered by compressed air cylinders while working in the restricted space, they moved the expedition's air compressor to the end of the breakwater and ran air lines directly down to their demand valves. This technique is known to divers as Hookah Diving because of the apparatus' resemblance to the traditional eastern smoking equipment. Our diving trio became so engrossed in their work that they kept at it all day without a break. The hypnotic effect of digging your own hole under water is one that many archaeological divers have experienced. The outside world becomes irrelevant, and all that seems to matter is the task of digging deeper and deeper down towards one's quarry. Our persistent three went on hour after hour and, as the day drew on, Elisha and I dived down to see how their work was progressing, but more particularly to plead with them to call it a day. But in vain. They were determined to go on, for this was their hole and they wanted to get to the bottom of it so all we could do was sustain them with the occasional bottle of Coca Cola and bananas. Feeding under water comes with experience, but I would not recommend it to the beginner.

At the end of the day our trio had completed their tasks and their work was well done, for they had revealed a small underwater room, a chamber in fact, which had been cut into the original bedrock, and its external face partially built up in stone. Standing in the centre of this chamber, the external wall curved partly over our heads to give the appearance of a domed ceiling.

On the following day we continued our excavation of the chamber using the air-lift to suck away the sand that remained on the bottom. Gradually, the floor of the chamber became revealed, and then to our surprise we uncovered a cannon ball, followed by another and yet another, until a complete group of perfectly clean cannon balls lay before us neatly stacked as though they had only been placed there the day before. Leading upwards from the submerged chamber was an oblique gallery cut into the rock face, the remains of a narrow staircase rising to a landing at sea level. This landing joined the bottom of a further flight of stairs leading to yet a higher level ten feet or so above the sea.

The stacked cannon balls and the level of the chamber suggested that it had been used as an arsenal, and this impression was confirmed when we found traces of blackened and charred material, evidence of fire. I think it likely that we had found the ammunition chamber which had blown up in Stopford's attack, and which is illustrated in the Victorian lithograph.

My interest in the Tower of Flies was now really stimulated and, when I returned home after the expedition, my research led me to the archives of the Palestine Exploration Fund. Here I came across a fascinating account of a naval battle during the times of the Third Crusade which revolved around the Tower of Flies. This account was written by Richard the Lionheart's chronicler, Geoffrey de Visnauf.

The year was 1189, and Acre had been captured by the great Arab Commander, Saladin. The city was now under siege from the Crusader forces and both the besieged and the besiegers were running out of provisions. The arrival of Moslem supply ships was eagerly awaited by both sides, for the capture of a Moslem ship could provide succour to the Crusaders, who were, if anything, worse off than the city's defenders. Visnauf's graphic account tells how the entrance to the harbour was barred by an iron chain which the defenders dropped just long enough to give access to the relief ships. He tells how a naval squadron composed of galleys, each propelled by two tiers of oars, charged towards the entrance of the harbour, whilst the Crusader galleys would race to head them off. One or two of the Arab ships slipped through to the safety of the harbour as the intercepting Crusader craft concentrated on overwhelming a less fortunate sister ship. 'In this naval contest,' Visnauf writes, 'the enemy lost a galley and a galleon together with their crews and our men, unhurt and joyful, gained a glorious triumph. Having drawn the captured galleys on shore they gave it up to be plundered by both sexes who came to meet them. On this our women dragged the Turks by the hair after treating them shamefully and cutting their throats in a disgraceful manner, and beheaded them and the weaker the hand to strike so much more lengthened the punishment inflicted for they used knives and not swords for cutting off their heads. A like sea fight was never seen, so destructive in its issue, accomplished with so much danger and completed with so much cost.' The writer continued with his account of the Siege of Acre and related how the Crusader Commander, having decided that it was impossible to starve the city to submission, resolved to attempt the capture of the harbour entrance which was the key to the control of the city. The double-banked galleys of the Crusader squadron were designed for speed, for each of the galleys from Pisa carried a hundred oars and in the bows the forecastle was crammed with men at arms, archers and the like. The larger of the galleys added a second castle amidships, with long overhanging projections to tangle with the enemy's rigging; a craft designed for ship-to-ship combat.

But the Crusader Commander had a problem, for the entrance to the harbour was dominated by the Tower of Flies. How to approach this fortress, let alone to overcome it, for the defenders were high above the decks of the attacking ships and appeared well nigh invincible? The ploy that the Commander decided upon was to have built on the deck of each galley a high wooden staging nearly equal in height to that of the Tower. From the top of this staging, missiles could be hurled directly at the highest level of the Tower. Specially constructed ladders were built for scaling the walls and the whole of the staging, including the deck of the galleys, was then sheathed in rawhide as an armour to resist missiles thrown down from the Tower.

Taking advantage of an early morning sea mist, the leather-clad Crusader galleys inched silently towards the Tower of Flies. A Moslem sentry peering into the mist could neither see nor hear them. Suddenly, with a mighty pull at the oars, the galleys shot out of the fog and with a splintering crash embedded themselves on to the Tower. Grappling irons were thrown and the attackers swarmed upon the decks of the galleys on to the tower's lowest ramparts, and in seconds the ladders were hoisted and the first Crusaders were scrambling to the top. In the words of the chronicler, 'The tower was assaulted for a long time with wonderful and intolerable violence; one party succeeded the other when tired, in rapid succession and with invincible valour. Darts flew with horrid crash, ponderous missiles rushed whizzing through the air.'

The Arab forces within the city itself, seeing the peril of their comrades on the tower, sent out their own boats to attack the Crusader galleys so that the latter were now having to fight on both flanks. The Crusaders, having made a foothold on the ramparts of the tower, had begun to gain the upper hand over the Moslems, who now retaliated by levering large rocks down on to the climbing attackers. These rocks were followed by Greek fire grenades which they hurled at the high staging of the galleys. Greek fire, a mixture of naphtha, saltpetre, sulphur and quicklime, was the incendiary weapon of the Greeks which had later been improved by the Byzantines and was still being used in the mediaeval period. The galleys' armour of hide, now gaping and torn, was no longer impervious to the missiles and the incendiary grenades. The attackers were horrified to look back and to see the staging below them crashing down on to the decks of the galleys, which in turn became gutted and capsized. The tower's defenders were 'overcome with excessive joy, laughed with loud shouts making a mockery of us and wagging their heads at our misfortune'.

I often find that the library can frequently be as exciting a hunting ground as the ancient archaeological site and, from time to time, a personal discovery from among old and dusty books can more than equal the unearthing of a relic from the past. This is how I feel about Geoffrey de Visnauf, for no analysis of the Tower of Flies can be complete without this author's narrative. But imagine my utter joy when I realised that Visnauf had solved a puzzle that had been worrying us on the dig ever since one of our divers recovered a strange-looking object from just beneath the sandy sea bed.

This was a small pineapple-like earthenware container some three-and-a-half inches long. But instead of having a normal opening in the top, it was surmounted by a small knob with a hole in it no more than an eighth of an inch in diameter. Its outside was decorated with an attractive striped and chequered pattern which had an Islamic look about it. This peculiar dark brown pineapple which rested very comfortably in the palm of the hand, was no ordinary container, for with its pointed bottom it could not stand up straight and, unlike an ordinary bottle or jar, it had no opening other than the tiny hole in the top.

Our enquiries in Israel had not got us very far. The general impression was that it was of mediaeval origin, and some thought that it might be a perfume container or maybe a sort of oil lamp, but neither of these views was acceptable, for why should one have a scent bottle or a lamp that could not stand up?

Some months after the Acre expedition, I heard from Arie Ben Elli that more pineapples have been found not far from Haifa. He now had a few in his museum and the letter was accompanied by two photographs. These showed pineapples of exactly the same dimensions, but with different, though equally attractive, decorations. Later that day I was due to attend a meeting of the British Government's Advisory Committee on Historic Wrecks, and I showed these photographs to a colleague, who was the Deputy Armourer of the Tower of London. His response was immediate; 'We haven't got any of these in the Tower, but I think I know what they are; they are very rare indeed, and they are probably a sort of petrol bomb.' 'But they didn't have petrol in the middle ages,' I said. 'No,' he replied, 'But they had Greek fire.' 'Greek fire?' – and then I remembered Visnauf's account of how Greek fire was used on the Tower of Flies. 'Gosh!' I thought, 'It's a Greek fire grenade; of course, why hadn't I thought of that before?' I was so excited that afternoon that I could hardly concentrate on the meeting. Later, confirmations came quick and fast. These were indeed Greek fire grenades, and the manner in which they were filled was by dipping into a tank of the incendiary mixture. The small hole in the top was designed to take a wick. The shape was perfectly suited for throwing and the weight, slightly more than that of a cricket ball, would enable the missile to be thrown a good fifty yards by hand, and double that distance by sling.

Elsewhere, Visnauf, in his itinerary of Richard I, has a great deal to say about Greek fire because this weapon played a big part in the Arabs' armoury. He tells of how grenades were smuggled into the besieged city of Acre by swimmers, and how one unfortunate fellow was caught. 'The man, being an expert swimmer, had already passed their (fishermen's) nets with a load which he carried suspended from his neck, for he had with him a skin of Greek fire, destined for the besieged in the city. In this way the Turks used to send Greek fire to the besieged by skilful swimmers, as they judged it the safest and most secret plan.' The hours of this noble band of Arab frogmen were limited, for the most skilful of them was also captured by the Crusaders and put to death. He was Ahsan-ul-Ghawasin, Issa as he was popularly known, and the ace swimmer who was reputed to have invented a 'breathing machine' with a bellows attached which enabled him to keep under the surface for long periods.

Our short expedition to Acre had proved fruitful, and in particular our discoveries had added to and illuminated some aspects of Acre's maritime history. Since then the Centre for Maritime Studies at Haifa University has continued with its diving and the survey of the harbour area combined with land excavations carried out by the same university's Department of Archaeology, and these digs are revealing daily the incredible history of this fascinating area.

VII

The Harbour of 'Magniloquent Hyperbole'

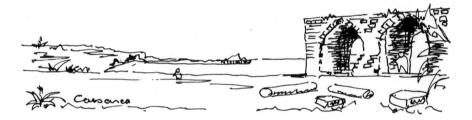

For thus saith the Lord God.
When I shall make thee a desolate city.
Like the cities that are not inhabited.
When I shall bring the deep upon you and great water shall
cover thee.'

EZEKIEL 27.19

There can be few tourists to Israel who have not visited Caesarea, for there are not many guided tours that do not include this site within their itineraries. Understandably so; for Caesarea, which lies on the Mediterranean coast about midway between Tel Aviv and Haifa, contains some of the finest monuments of the Roman, Byzantine and Crusader periods.

Here we can wander through the Crusader city, its perimeter wall, bastions and moat still in a fine state of preservation. Just outside the Crusader walls lies the 5th-century Byzantine church with its delightful bird and animal mosaic floor, and then, to my mind the most splendid of the remains, those from the city built by King Herod in 13 BC – the delightful Roman theatre, now skilfully mended and used for open air concerts, and the site of the only known contemporary slab inscribed with the name Pontius Pilate. I have walked the whole length of the Roman aqueduct now mostly covered by sand dunes. The structure was originally built to convey fresh water to Caesarea, a distance of some eight miles. And then there are the recently excavated, beautifully built, round towers of Herod's Caesarea: Roman masonry at its best.

The remains of Herod's city are to be seen everywhere; sherds scatter the shoreline and it is not uncommon for the casual beach stroller to spot a Roman coin or an amulet from a necklace. These remnants of Herod's Caesarea have remained to be seen, but the greatest of the city's features has now vanished entirely from sight. The Great Harbour of Caesarea, known as Sebastos, was reputed to be one of the largest in the Mediterranean. It disappeared from sight so long ago that 19th-century travellers doubted whether it had ever existed at all.

Until recently all that we knew of the harbour was based on one literary source, that of *The War of the Jews* by Josephus Flavius. Josephus relates how King Herod had rebuilt the Temple in Jerusalem, and then embarked on a lavish programme of embellishing his country with palaces and fortresses, the most famous of which was that at Massada in the Judean Desert. His greatest ambition, however, was to build a major port on the Mediterranean and one that could compare in size and splendour with those of his Roman patrons. At that time the only working port into Palestine was at Jaffa, and this was so poorly sheltered that mariners were unable to put into it unless the sea was more or less calm. Herod's problem was that his coastline was straight and totally lacking in natural anchorages or creeks. But he was determined to have his port, even if he had to build it artificially and entirely from scratch.

He selected a site more or less equidistant from his northern and southern borders, at a small settlement originally founded by the Phoenicians called Stratos Tower. The port and the city took twelve years to build and Herod named it after the Roman Emperor, Augustus. Josephus, who visited the city twelve years after its completion, describes a metropolis of glistening white limestone laid out on a grid, its main streets leading to the great harbour and the presence of many fountains supplied with fresh water. The vast harbour, he said, had a mole two hundred feet broad, half of which formed a breakwater while the other half consisted of arched dwellings for the sailors. These were all enclosed in a broad walk which stretched out to sea in a vast semi-circle. Above the breakwater was a further wall and from this arose at regular intervals a whole series of large towers. The harbour entrance faced north where the winds were less severe, and the entrance was flanked on each side by massive plinths, each surmounted by three gigantic statues. On the breakwater, Herod had built a temple dedicated to Caesar, and inside this temple stood a giant statue of the Emperor modelled on the Zeus of Olympia.

This was the account of Herod's Caesarea that was handed down to travellers and explorers, and so one can imagine their consternation when they stood on the shores of Caesarea and, instead of seeing a giant harbour, saw only the small, pathetic remains of a Crusader jetty. Claude Conder was one such explorer who came here in 1873. Conder's credentials were impeccable for he was the Director of the Palestine Exploration Fund's Survey of Western Palestine. The perplexed Conder wrote: 'At Caesarea we are brought face to face with the question – the reliability of Josephus . . . Here at Caesarea we have a description of the port and public buildings which contain undoubted inaccuracies; he represents the port as equal in size to Piraeus but it measures scarcely two hundred yards across either way, whilst the famous harbour at Athens was three quarters of a mile long and over six hundred yards in breadth.'

Equally sceptical was a contemporary of Conder's, the Reverend W D Thomson. Mr Thomson, self-styled 'Thirty Years a Missionary in Syria and Palestine', was less charitable than Conder. Of the harbour remains he wrote, 'Look at them and then turn to Josephus and see if you can discover any resemblance. Beyond all doubt, much of that description is magniloquent Josephian hyperbole. Who can read of a mole two hundred feet broad built of stones more than fifty feet long, eighteen feet wide and nine feet deep without a smile? Why, the whole harbour encircled by it is not much broader.'

103

There is no doubt that Josephus has shown himself to be prone to exaggeration. Mount Tabor, for example, is a plateau which he describes as three miles long and twenty thousand feet high, but in fact it is two miles long and one thousand eight hundred feet high. But there was a deeper and more subtle reason why the 19th century was very suspicious of Josephus. Josephus, by his own admission, had been a traitor. During the rebellion of the Jews against the Romans in the 1st century, Josephus had been the Commander of the Jewish Forces in the Gallilean sector. By a devious method, he managed to save his own life while all but one of his men were slain, and, in surrendering to the enemy, gained the favour of Vespasian, the Roman General, who bestowed upon him Roman Citizenship. Joseph Ben Matthias, as he was then known, switched his alliance and henceforth was known as Josephus Flavius. In his writings, Josephus passionately defends his actions, but in the eyes of many he doth protest too much, and was a traitor who went out of his way to glorify the Romans and Herod. In the eyes of the 19th century, Josephus was not to be trusted, and this distrust of the man himself extended to his writings.

This idea of the harbour that never was, prevailed right into the mid-20th century until 1960. In that year, a motor yacht, *The Sea Diver*, dropped anchor at Caesarea after a twenty-nine-day voyage from Puerto Rico. Aboard was its owner, Edwin Link, the American industrialist, known as the inventor of the Link Trainer to all World War Two airmen. Link, having made his fortune, decided to spend the rest of his years as an undersea explorer, and he built his specially commissioned boat, *The Sea Diver*, for that purpose.

Having investigated the sunken city of Port Royal in Jamaica, Link then turned his interest to the mystery of the missing harbour at Caesarea. The task he set himself was to search the sea bottom for any signs of an ancient harbour – possibly its foundations, masonry, indeed anything which could shed light on this controversial subject. And he was joined by Elisha and Chaim Stav and other Israeli divers, working under the Archaeological Department of the University of Jerusalem.

Link, who was after all a flyer before becoming a diver, also wanted to see Caesarea from the air as well as from below the sea. The sea was exceptionally calm on the day that Link took off from the Haifa airstrip in a light plane. He was accompanied by Louis Marden, the chief photographer of the *National Geographic Magazine*. They arrived over Caesarea and, looking down into the sea, saw below them the shadow of a vast, semi-circular submerged structure sweeping out to sea from the shore and then back again. This semi-circular ring was unbroken except for a gap in the north west. Marden took a series of photographs which are still classics of their kind and, armed with these, Link's divers proceeded to search the structure which had shown up on the aerial photographs. The finding of man-made masonry blocks at a depth of twenty-seven feet, together with the photographic evidence, proved that Link had discovered the remains of the harbour described by Josephus and, what is more, he showed that the harbour was very large indeed.

Three years later, I, in company with Joe Shaw, Chaim Stav and Shuka Shapira, dived on what was once the entrance to the harbour of Caesarea. The gigantic blocks of masonry that I viewed through my mask as we floated down, were quite the largest that I have ever seen underwater. Lying all in a heap, rather like a child's building blocks, it was just as if we were diving through the ruins of some palace that had, in antiquity, been engulfed by the sea. As for the blocks themselves, the largest was thirty-six feet long by ten feet wide by ten feet deep, and there were three others measuring twenty feet long by eight feet square, and many others fourteen feet long. So precarious seemed these blocks, that I had the uncomfortable feeling that they could collapse on us at any moment.

We followed Chaim southwards along the line of the submerged breakwater and the sea bed below resembled the remains of a demolished building from which everything had been cleared except the foundations and bases. The sand had spread itself over the now unrecognisable remains of some sort of structure, but every now and then Chaim would point out the barely discernible profile of a building block. Everywhere there were scattered remains of Roman pottery; sherds and broken jar handles by the hundred, either lying loosely, or firmly embedded in rock formations. All this indicated a great amount of building work, but its form was so unidentifiable that I doubted the possibility of attempting anything like a survey of this jungle of rubble.

But a little further on along the route we came across Chaim, who was by now sitting astride something on the sea bed. As we came up closer we found that his seat was, in fact, a quite perfect long wall formed of about fifteen immaculately-shaped blocks laid quite straight, and in a form which would have done justice to any mediaeval cathedral. Each block was about three feet long by two feet wide, and they were in perfect condition. Further on, there were similar stretches of wall and, as Joe and I conversed silently, but with signals and gestures, we asked ourselves, 'Was it possible that immaculate masonry of this sort could be laid at a depth of twenty-seven to thirty feet?' This was a question that had been puzzling us for years, and it was not until quite recently that my old friend Dr Nicholas Flemming came up with the answer.

Nick, who had already established his reputation in the archaeological world some years before, by his survey of the sunken city of Appellonia in North Africa, is a geologist who has used archaeological observation as a means to the measuring of the movements of shorelines since Neolithic times. At the invitation of Elisha, Nick had accepted a short-term visiting professorship at Haifa University, and it was in the course of his coastal survey, that he discovered a geological fault at Caesarea, showing that the whole of the harbour structure had been caused to slip, no doubt by an earthquake. Many earthquakes along the Levant coastline have been recorded in historical writings, but it was never known whether any of these had drastically affected the harbour at Caesarea. Nick had now clearly shown that this was the case. Certainly the earthquake would have had the effect of demolishing a great deal of the architectural superstructure, and the gigantic scattered blocks of the harbour entrance can be taken as evidence of such a catastrophic collapse.

As the reader will have gathered by now, my underwater exploring seems to act as a catalyst for further research, and I find myself becoming absorbed in the area in which I have dived, and in the discoveries that have been made. And so it has been with Caesarea for, having visited this place frequently and having dived on the lost harbour, I became intrigued by the history of the harbour and, more specifically, I kept asking myself how was it that such a gigantic

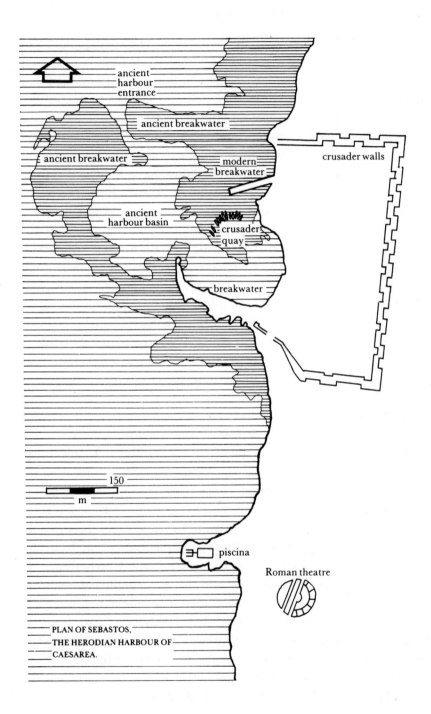

ancient harbour entrance

ancient breakwater

ancient breakwater

modern breakwater

crusader walls

ancient harbour basin

crusader quay

breakwater

150

m

piscina

Roman theatre

PLAN OF SEBASTOS, THE HERODIAN HARBOUR OF CAESAREA.

structure could be almost totally eliminated. The earthquake alone could not have accounted for this, for tens of thousands of tons of superstructure, instead of just lying on the sea bottom, had just vanished into thin air.

First its history. There is no doubt that in its first years, Caesarea was a major and flourishing port, for it is mentioned in the New Testament as being the place that saw Peter first preaching to the Gentiles at the invitation of the Roman Centurion, Cornelius. Saint Paul landed there in AD 49, and subsequently left for Rome in AD 60. The city was the scene of the first Jewish uprising which was soon to grow into total war between the Jews and the Romans, a conflict that Josephus related so vividly. He tells how the Roman General, Vespasian, having proved his skill as a suppressor of rebelling subjects by his crushing of the Britons, was summoned to Palestine, and it was to Caesarea that he came with his crack legions. Vespasian advanced north taking toll of the fragmented Jewish forces, sacking Jerusalem and overcoming Massada after its epic resistance. He returned to Caesarea with thousands of Jewish captives who were put to death in the Hippodrome. Two years later Vespasian was declared Emperor in the same city which by now had become the capital of Palestine; its new name – Colonia Prima Flavia Augustus Caesarensis.

I was reminded of this link between vanquished Judea and defeated Britain shortly after my return following my first trip to Israel. When we visited Caesarea with Elisha and Pnina, we ended our day in the restaurant overlooking the beach. Elisha pointed out that Vespasian could not have wished for a better military port and base from which to launch his campaign. On our return to England I found waiting for me an invitation from Professor Barry Cunliffe asking that I visit his excavation of the Roman Palace at Fishbourne, near Chichester.

Trudie, my daughter Barbara and I were conducted over the excavation by Professor Cunliffe, and then, knowing of my interest in ancient harbours, he pointed out that Fishbourne had been an important Channel port in Roman times. 'I have no doubt,' he said, 'that the Emperor Vespasian used the excellent anchorage here at Fishbourne to house his invasion fleet in AD 43.'

It is clear that Caesarea continued as Roman Palestine's main port for a great number of years, and it is even referred to quite frequently in the Talmud. The city, in fact, housed one of the major schools of Jewish learning alongside a centre of early Christian study which in later years was to blossom into a fully-grown bishopric. However, by the 6th century the harbour had by all accounts fallen into disuse. In a report written by Procopius of Gaza, the following appears: 'Since the port of the city named after Caesar had fallen into bad condition in the course of time, and was open to every threat of the sea and no longer, in fact, deserved to be classed as a port, but retained from its former fortune merely a name, you did not overlook her need and her constant laments over the ships which frequently escaping the sea were wrecked in the harbour.'

Although efforts were made in those years to repair the harbour, it seems that it had seen its last days.

In 638 the city fell to the Arab armies and, although the harbour was now no longer used, the city itself continued to flourish and the freshwater aqueduct built by the Romans was a boon to the Arab horticulturalists, who turned the maritime port into a garden city of exotic plants and cool fountains. Mukaddisi, the Arab traveller, extolled, 'There is no city more beautiful nor any better filled with good things . . . its lands are excellent and its fruits delicious.' But the harbour which once housed great Roman fleets, now saw nothing more than the occasional fishing dhow. However, earthquakes and drifting sands and dunes could not in themselves have totally swept the harbour away, for none of these factors together would have been sufficient to eliminate this vast marine structure. The explanation of the harbour's total disappearance is that man himself gave the *coup de grâce* by deliberately and systematically dismantling the remains of the breakwater stone by stone. The ruins of Caesarea were turned into a giant warehouse of architectural stonework. Columns of porphyry and syenite, originally brought from Egypt, elaborately carved capitals, moulded and carved entablatures, tens of thousands of tons of ashlar blocks, were loaded on to boats and transported for the construction of other cities.

The stonework of Caesarea was taken to every part of the eastern Mediterranean; the gracious Khan El Ourdan at Acre was built

109

entirely from columns from Caesarea and Peter Throckmorton, the marine archaeologist, told me that he had found off the shore of Italy a sunken wreck containing columns precisely matching in size and materials those which he had seen at Caesarea, and he strongly suspected that they had come from that city.

Rose Macaulay in her *The Pleasure of Ruins* writes, 'To track down the ancient splendours of Caesarea one would have to explore the buildings of a whole region, for it had served as a quarry furnishing costly shafts and ready-made blocks and capitals for not only the builders of the middle ages, but for recent pashas who could use the vast remains within their reach to rear palaces, fountains and mosques.' The fate of the harbour's great breakwaters is now clear, for what could be easier than to moor a boat alongside the mole where the blocks of the structure itself could be prised off and loaded aboard. Thus each valuable squared block was wrenched from the walls until even those below water level had been scavenged. The vast semi-circular pattern of the harbour's breakwaters can still be seen from the air when the sea is calm; it is made up of those foundation blocks too difficult to lift and the collapsed superstructure now overgrown with concretion.

This is the story of Sebastos, the harbour of Caesarea, how it came to be built, forgotten and then rediscovered. Yet from the archaeologist's point of view, this is only the beginning of the story. When Elisha Linder first asked me to dive with him at Caesarea together with Joe Shaw, we prepared a report in which we recommended a full-scale survey of the sunken harbour linked to a foreshore survey which we anticipated would extend over many seasons. In my notes leading to the report, I made this observation: 'One thing that we understand about the harbour at Caesarea and about no other Roman harbour is that we know from the writing of Josephus precisely when it was built; from the years 22 BC to its completion in 9 BC. Land archaeological sites are generally dated by stratigraphical methods, pottery, etc; but these methods are difficult on harbour sites and one has to resort to dating from architectural styles, constructional systems and similar imprecise methods. So little is known about ancient marine construction that one can be centuries out in attempting a chronology by these methods. But because we have the exact dating of Caesarea, the detailed analysis of this harbour is an important basis for the overall study of ancient harbour construction.'

The organisation and finances needed for a project of this sort were considerable and, as the years went by, I was forced to the view that the Caesarea project would never come to fruition and that the techniques that went to building this vast Roman harbour would remain a submerged secret.

But I was wrong, for in 1979 I received a letter from Elisha Linder informing me that his Centre for Maritime Studies at Haifa University had at last launched its Caesarea project under the name of the Caesarea Ancient Harbour Excavation Project (CAHEP). Dr Avner Raban, Elisha's deputy, was to be its joint director with Robert L Hohlfelder of the University of Colorado as his co-director. This project has continued every year since then and each season has produced new evidence of the extraordinary level of sophisticated engineering used by Herod's engineers. One discovery that I personally found exciting was the revealing of timber beams and shuttering by which the harbour walls were constructed beneath the surface. The reason for my personal interest related to my early years as a student when I became absorbed in the works of Vitruvius, the Roman architect, whose treatise was essential reading for any student of Roman classical architecture. To this day I cannot avoid cringing when I see a so-called Roman capitol and column which deviates in the slightest form from the precise delineations as laid down by Vitruvius in his Orders of Architecture. But Vitruvius wrote not only on architecture, but also on civil engineering and his paper on harbours, breakwaters and shipyards contains precise specifications on submerged harbour walls including the timber and shuttering to be used in their construction. The timbers that were found in the lowest parts of the Caesarea harbour walls corresponded very closely to the specifications laid down by Vitruvius.

Last year I returned once again to dive on this vast underwater site and I was shown so much that I was not able to see on our first visit some fifteen years before. Pointed out to me was very clear evidence of an inner harbour; of a secondary wall running parallel to the out-side face of the moles presumably to act as a wave-breaker and a sophisticated system of channels containing grooves cut into the rock to hold wooden sluice gates for the controlling of water flow. These were all part of a system to permit the harbour to be flushed out, thus preventing silting.

I never fail to be humbled when I come across yet another example of the ingenuity and artistry of builders in antiquity. Sebastos at Caesarea is a most extraordinary specimen of Roman maritime engineering skill and I concur so much with Avner Raban's statement: 'This Herodian port is an example of a 21st century harbour built two thousand years ago. In fact, if the modern harbours of Ashdod and Haifa had employed such systems of design and engineering, they would not have had the problems they face today.'

VIII

Two Roman Fishtanks

Thine eyes like the fishpools in Heshbon, by the gate of Bath-rabbim.

SONG OF SOLOMON 7.4

To drown in eighteen inches of water is a cruel enough fate for anyone. If the victim were to be a diver of experience it would, to say the least, seem curious. But I had an added embarrassment, for at that time I was the Chairman of the British Sub-Aqua Club and it was that, probably more than anything else, that saved me. In gathering that one last moment of strength that saved them from the jaws of death, some have been said to be spurred by the image of their loved ones, or being too young to die – a desperate will to live. In my case it was vanity! Sheer vanity! I could not bear the thought of that headline . . . '*Top* British diver drowns in puddle'.

The year was 1969 and the place Lapithos, better known nowadays as Lambousa on the north coast of Cyprus some eight miles west of Kyrenia. On the beach at the very water's edge lies a large rectangular stone pool. It looks like a swimming pool, but is actually a Roman fishtank. At the end of this tank, against the sea, is a nicely built stone structure a couple of feet high, with two narrow tunnels leading from the tank into the sea. This fishtank, or *piscina*, was an important find for me, and I had just about finished surveying it. All that remained to be done was to take the internal dimensions of the tunnels. The tank was full of water and the tunnels, which measured about twenty inches square, led directly from the tank into the sea. I found, however, that these were heavily silted in sand, and whereas one was completely submerged, the other tunnel did have just a few inches of air space between its roof and the surface of the water. With the aid of a mask and a snorkel I was able to crawl into the tunnel, take a measurement or two, and then push myself back out of the tunnel so that I could put these measurements on to my drawing pad. This process went on quite well and little by little I went deeper into the tunnel, until eventually I had crawled right to the end where it was completely blocked. However, I found that the sand here was quite loose and by a bit of shovelling with my hands I was able to reveal more of the tunnel's stone interior.

My breathing was not too difficult because the mouth of my snorkel was in the air space just under the roof of the tunnel, and although the air was becoming a bit warm I could just about get sufficient to keep me going. Having taken my final measurements, I pushed forward with my hands against the end of the tunnel to enable me to slide out backwards, and then came the first rude shock. I could not move. I pushed again harder, but without success. I seemed to be stuck fast. The sand which I had shovelled from the end of the tunnel had somehow built up under my stomach and this had the effect of acting as a sort of wedge.

At that moment I was really quite calm and felt that I had better think this thing out. But as I did so, I began, with some apprehension, to realise the extent of my predicament, for here I was, by myself, stuck fast, head first into a cavity which was rapidly becoming very hot and extremely uncomfortable. The beach was deserted and there was absolutely no point in calling out. What is more, I felt my head beginning to ache, and then I realised of course, that if I was wedged tight in the tunnel this would also have the effect of preventing very much fresh air from getting in from the open end.

Then I began to feel sick and suddenly I became cold and trembled. I realised in near-panic that if I passed out my head would drop, the snorkel would fill with water and I would drown. 'Is this the way it is going to happen?' I thought. I cannot pretend that my life flashed before my eyes; all that I could think of was that it was too darned ridiculous for words, that this could not happen to me of all people, and then I saw these bizarre and lurid headlines again: – 'BS-AC Chairman dies in ancient Roman fishtank.' Even in death I could not face the shame of it and in one desperate, frantic, final effort I pushed until I screamed. I felt the packed sand beneath me suddenly run, and with one final shove I popped out like a champagne cork into the cool waters of the tank. The waves broke against the tunnel's superstructure and sprayed over me and I gulped in the fresh air; it had never tasted so sweet and I remember that I began to laugh – well, it was not really laughter, it was more like crying.

But I should like to get back to the fishtank itself and tell you more about this. I happened to be in Cyprus in 1969 advising on the possibility of an hotel and housing project, and at the same time I had received an invitation from Professor Michael Katzev to go and dive with him on his underwater excavation of a 4th-century BC wreck at Kyrenia. I shall always remember Katzev's project as being a model of its kind, an example to all underwater archaeologists. The wreck lay a few hundred yards out to sea from Kyrenia Castle and was at a depth of a hundred and twenty feet. The water was so clear that when I stood on the barge moored over the site I could actually see the divers working on the bottom, and the outline of part of the already excavated wreck. Michael accompanied me over the site with its hundreds of amphorae lying on their sides neatly stacked, and the skeleton and timbers of the ship virtually intact. The excavation was being undertaken by an international team of divers, with an abundance of technical aids such as stereoscopic underwater cameras, bottom-to-surface telephone communications, and even an underwater telephone booth. This was a plastic dome anchored some five feet above the sea bottom and filled with compressed air which forced the water level down to the bottom of the dome, leaving the interior of the dome itself as an air space. When Michael and I wanted to converse, we simply swam to the dome, popped up inside and took off our masks. Michael eventually recovered the whole wreck, with its contents, and this can be seen in Kyrenia Castle in a special museum.

One afternoon I returned from the Kyrenia wreck to the nearby hotel where Trudie and I were staying. She said, 'I've been walking along the beach and I found something which I think might interest you.' She took me to where she had been, and there on the beach was our large fishtank. It was a really fine specimen with channels going off diagonally from each side into additional smaller fishtanks, and then further along there were more tanks adding up to five in all. What excited me was that, although I had studied fishtanks in Italy where there are many fine examples, this was quite the largest complex that I had ever seen outside the Roman homeland. As we were leaving the following day there was little time other than to take some photographs and odd dimensions, but this did not worry me unduly as I assumed that this complex had been well documented.

On our way back to the airport, we had time to drop into the Museum in Nicosia to see Dr Nicolaou, the Deputy Director of the Department of Antiquities and, when I mentioned these fishtanks, I was astonished to hear that although Nicolaou knew of their existence they had not, in fact, been documented, and that really very little was known about them. In reply to my request Dr Nicolaou said that, as no excavation would be involved, he would be pleased to give me authority to survey the complex, and kindly agreed to contribute an historical background if my surveys proved fruitful.

Later that year I had to return to Cyprus on business, and it was then that I took the opportunity to steal three days at the end of my visit to enable me to carry out the fishtank survey. You may well ask what is it that is so interesting about Roman fishtanks? For compared with temples and Roman baths, theatres and colosseums, and even submerged Roman harbours, fishtanks must be of comparatively minor interest. But strange as it may seem, this small and specialised area of Roman ingenuity is fascinating, and quite worthy of study.

Two Roman Fishtanks

The best of these installations are naturally seen in Italy itself, and particularly on the west coast where they come in all shapes and sizes: oblong, circular, semi-circular and octagonal. These installations are sometimes quite mistakenly called fish farms, but they are not that because they were used by the Romans not for breeding, but only for the storage of sea fish. The fish, after being caught were taken immediately to the fishtanks, which were so located and designed as to ensure a continuous circulation of fresh sea water. The expertise developed in the design of these tanks was considerable, and I had become increasingly fascinated by the ingenuity shown by their designers. For example, the channels which feed the sea water into the tanks have complicated sluices built into their sides, so that the flow of water can be controlled precisely. Some of these installations have compartments at different depths, to accommodate various types of fish, and it is clear that the designers had located the tanks in positions which would take full advantage of local tides, wind directions and wave patterns.

Almost invariably these tanks were built adjoining coastal villas, thus providing their owners with a continuous supply of fresh fish, even when sea conditions prevented normal fishing. Contemporary writers of the period relate how these *piscinae* very soon became status symbols, and their owners would vie with one another in the size and style of their installations, and it was not long before the *piscina* became as essential an addition to the seaside villa as the swimming pool is to the present-day Florida home.

As the *piscinae* became more imposing, they took on the form of aquaria rather than simple storage tanks. The *piscina* had now become something of a fashion for the high-born rich, whom Cicero the Roman writer dubbed *Piscinari* – fishponders. The agricultural writer Varro was equally scathing of his friend Quintas Hortensius, 'Who would never eat the contents of his pond but instead, sent to Pulteoli Market for the fish for his table and, if any of his *piscina* fish was sick, he was even more attentive to them than he was to his sick slaves.' Marshall writes with, I suspect, some journalistic cynicism of Apollinaris who, 'Could always furnish his table no matter the stormy sea by letting down his line from his bed or couch to catch turbot or bass.'

The Roman writers do tend to highlight the eccentrics, and hence the many tales of excesses among the *Piscinari*. But these anecdotes do make amusing reading. For example, Marshall writes of one owner who had eels and mullets who would answer to their master's call and another writer, Achion, has a story of a Roman who had a female murena which he adorned with a jewelled necklace and earrings, and which also came to him when he called, and when she died he wept and buried her. And there is also the well-known story of Vedius Pollio who fattened his murena on delinquent slaves; and of the Emperor Domitian who kept pet fish that would come up at the sound of their master's voice and lick his hand.

The Lapithos Roman fishtank site is, as far as I am aware, the largest and most impressive complex of its sort yet discovered outside the Italian homeland. Its significance as far as Biblical archaeology is concerned, is that Cyprus is one of the Lands of the Bible: 'They made your deck of pine from the coast of Cyprus,' we read in Ezekiel and it was from Cyprus, the 'Copper Island', that this material was imported into Palestine. As far as this narrative is concerned, my link of Roman Cyprus with Roman Palestine is forged by the fishtanks at Lapithos and a very similar installation of, I believe, the same vintage of Caesarea.

If you stand on the uppermost tier of the theatre at Caesarea and look out to sea, you will see a small promontory which juts out from the shore. On a stormy day most of it will be submerged by the surging waves, but when the sea is calm it is possible to walk all over it and to examine the large *piscina* which sits comfortably in its centre. Leading out from this large tank can be seen water supply channels precisely similar in type to those at the Lapithos *piscina* and if one looks closely, it is possible to make out the lines of additional supplementary tanks which are linked by channels to the main central tank. Around the tank are remains of quite substantial walls, and paved terraces.

Curiously, not only is there an architectural resemblance between this site and that at Lapithos, but their traditional names are also very close, for the Caesarea *piscina* is known as 'Brechat Cleopatra' – The Bath of Cleopatra – and the folklore name for Lapithos is The Bath of the Queen. I had first come across this site with Dr Joseph Shaw on our reconnaissance of Caesarea many years before, but on that occasion I was only able to make a sketch or two and take a few photographs, and it had long been my wish to come back to this site and to survey it in detail.

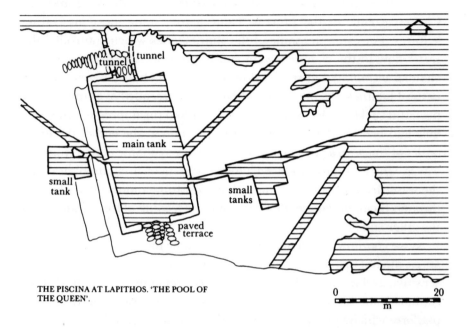

THE PISCINA AT LAPITHOS. 'THE POOL OF THE QUEEN'.

My opportunity came about in sad circumstances. The Yom Kippur War struck Israel in 1973 and Elisha wrote to me with the news that his son-in-law, a fighter pilot, had been killed in the first day of the conflict, and that three of our diving companions on the Tanit Expedition at Shave Zion had also fallen. I had spent so many rewarding and enjoyable hours with these people, my friends, and I felt now that I wanted to return to see if I could comfort them in their sorrow. So it was that Trudie and I, in October of that year, sat with Elisha and Pnina Linder once more in their home on Kibbutz Maagan Michael, and we wept.

Our time was spent going from town to town and talking with people. There was hardly a family that had not been touched by this and previous wars, and towards the end of our stay Trudie and I felt emotionally drained. A few days rest was called for before returning to England and we booked ourselves in at a small holiday villa at Caesarea. It was then that I remembered Brechat Cleopatra, and I told Trudie of my interest in this site. 'Well,' she replied, 'here's your chance, and I'll come along and help you.'

We spent two contented days measuring and drawing Brechat Cleopatra and, in the process, came across some most interesting features. For example, some of the sluice stones which controlled the water flow in the channels were still in position, and in one case the channel terminated at sea level into a hole which was bored into the natural bedrock. As the waves advanced and recoiled over this hole, a powerful sucking effect was created, and I had the impression that this hole had been bored precisely in this position at the end of the main outlet of the *piscina*. Its effect was to create a syphonic action from the waves, which in turn produced a forced system of circulation, drawing the water from the extract channel and creating a movement of water through the main *piscina*, thus assisting the feeding of fresh water from the other end of the tank.

As we continued with our survey, it became more apparent that this *piscina* did not just have a utilitarian purpose, but contained elements of sensitive architectural design. There were remains of column drums, capitals, and in the centre of the *piscina* there was placed a large platform which may well have been the base of a statue.

On the very last morning of our survey, we had more or less completed our task; the sun was now high and we were looking forward to a long, cool drink. We collected our surveying gear together and I thanked Trudie for her assistance; she replied that it would have been nice to have found 'A little coin or something like that.' At that moment I leant over to pick up my satchel and my eye was caught by a spot of colour in the sand. I casually flicked the spot with my shoe and another fragment of colour emerged beside the first. Putting down my satchel I lightly brushed my fingers across the surface of the sand to reveal a small portion of pink and black terracotta mosaic. Further brushing revealed more mosaic. By then Trudie was kneeling by my side. 'I wish I had a small brush,' I said. 'But I've got one,' replied Trudie, diving into her handbag and extracting her brand new and expensive hairbrush. To my enquiring look she replied, 'Oh, what the hell!' and within a short time we had revealed an area of mosaic terrace nearly the size of a table tennis table. It was a splendid geometric design composed of pink, black and white *tesserae* within a border, and outside this border was the beginning of a similar mosaic predominantly of white *tesserae* with regularly spaced, small, black motifs. We could hardly believe our luck, for our discovery had probably been made possible by the fact that two days before there had been torrential rain storms on the coast, and this had washed away most of the covering sand, leaving only a thin layer.

Dismissing all thoughts of refreshment, we continued for the rest of the afternoon to clean the mosaic, brushing away the sand, and then gently watering it with the aid of my faithful expedition hat which now served as a bucket. We photographed the terrace from every angle and then took measurements and I was delighted to discover that the mosaic terrace was placed directly on the central axis of the large *piscina*, and was, therefore, an integral part of the whole *piscina* design. We went as far with our cleaning as we could, but there were areas covered by large boulders which we were unable to move, so we covered over the whole area with as thick a protective layer of sand as we could, and on the next day travelled to Jerusalem to report our find to Dr Avraham Biran, the Director of the Department of Antiquities.

While we told Avraham of our find, his photographer took our films to his darkroom for printing. Within a short time he returned, together with my old friend Dr Moshe Dothan, who was then Deputy Director. He and Avraham agreed that the mosaic was a rare example of the Herodian period, and clearly dated from Herod's Caesarea. Avraham and Moshe were delighted for us, and I promised them that I would complete the drawings from my survey and, together with the photographs, publish these as soon as possible. In the following year my paper appeared in the Israel Exploration Journal.

Our work at Brechat Cleopatra remains with me as a particularly nostalgic memory, principally because Trudie was able to share with me that rare moment of archaeological discovery. The existence of the mosaic had not been known, and we had found it together. In my travels I have been lucky to have had many similar experiences, but Trudie's enjoyment of these had, before Caesarea, been mostly second-hand, and now for the first time she was able to enjoy this magical moment for herself.

The Caesarea *piscina* raises two interesting developments of thought. The first relates to what I wrote previously about the Roman *piscina*, more often than not, being identified closely with the site of a coastal villa. If this theory applies equally to Caesarea, then the architectural character of the *piscina* would lead one to think that its associated villa would have been equally as distinctive. It follows, therefore, that in the building of Caesarea, Herod himself would almost certainly have built a seaside villa for his own use, and I would suspect therefore that if such a villa ever existed, then it would be located very close to the *piscina*. This is an area of study which I have been unable to pursue myself, but I hope that others might be able to develop this idea.

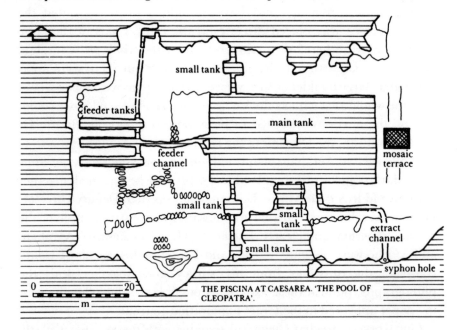

THE PISCINA AT CAESAREA. 'THE POOL OF CLEOPATRA'.

Another problem revealed by the *piscina* relates to that of coastal movement in the Caesarea area. One of the interesting aspects of Brechot Cleopatra is that its level in relation to the sea must be very close indeed to that which existed two thousand years ago when it was first built. I have no doubt that with some clearance and reconstruction the *piscina* would be able to function as it did originally. In my chapter on the submerged harbour of Caesarea, the reader will recall our discovery of stone walls at a depth of thirty feet, and at the time of that discovery I had, on the basis of the level of the *piscina* only some three hundred yards to the south, assumed that there had been no land movement in the harbour site, and that therefore the walls must have been constructed underwater by divers with considerable skill. It was a difficult assumption to make, but the evidence seemed to speak for itself. It was not, however, until some years later that Dr Nick Flemming produced evidence of a tectonic movement of land on the site of the harbour, of such a local nature that, whereas the harbour itself sank, the *piscina* which stood just nearby, remained at its original level.

IX

The Diver in the Bible

Thy way is in the sea and thy path in the great waters.

PSALMS 77.20

A few years ago I joined a party of students and staff from Elisha's Haifa University department in an archaeological tour of some of the islands in the Aegean. I met their boat, a converted fishing craft, in Rhodes and we went on to Simi, Cos, Kalimnos, Delos, Santorin and Crete. What more can one ask for than to sail these ancient waters, often in the company of delightfully inquisitive dolphins, to be able to dive, study and to sketch and then in the cool evening to talk, and with the aid of the local brew, to permit the tongue to loosen and the mind to soar?

It was on one such evening that we sat outside a small taverna by the harbour in Kalimnos. Kalimnos is the home of the sponge divers, the Kalimnian divers who, in the spring, sail as far as the north African

124

coast and then return in October with their cargoes of sponges to a noisy welcome. It was May, and the sponge fleet was away, but there sat with us an old man who had been a hard hat diver before the days of the aqualung. I suppose that he was not really much older than me, but he was bent and crippled by the bends and he looked old indeed. His English was quite good; he said that he had picked it up during the last war and we talked into the early hours about his sponge diving. Well, he did most of the talking, and we just listened enthralled. He claimed that his great-great-grandfather was one of the divers who went from Kalimnos to Cithern in 1802 to salvage some of the Elgin Marbles which had sunk in *The Brigadier Mentor* on her way to England.

When one of our group told the old diver that he had been born in Jerusalem, the old man's eyes filled with tears. He said that he had been a devout man all his life and that it was only with God's help that he was able to cope with his affliction; that it had been his lifelong wish to go to the Holy Land, particularly to the Sea of Galilee, but this would never now be possible. And then he said something that moved us all profoundly. 'You know, my friends, I have been a sponge diver all my life since I was a little boy and it has brought me much pain. But when Jesus was on the cross they put a sponge soaked in spirit in His mouth to help His agony. Somehow to know this helps me in my agony as well.'

The next day before we left, we saw the old diver again sitting by his sponge stall. I picked what I thought was a good specimen to take home to Trudie, but the old man stayed my hand. He replaced the sponge in its tray and from below the stall produced a splendid large semi-spherical sponge, far better than any that he had on display. 'You are a diver, my friend, and this is one you must have for the same price. You will have it for ever.' The old man was true to his word, for I still have this sponge and it is as good as the day I bought it.

What the old diver said about Jesus and the sponge set me off on a line of research which I have found extremely rewarding. The sponge is frequently mentioned in the New Testament and so too are pearls. The sponge and the pearl are riches of the sea that can only be retrieved from the deep by the diver and no one else. But, as yet, as far as I am able to discover, the diver is never named or referred to in the Bible though it is certain that diving in deep waters must have been practised by the Bible people. There is, in fact, a hint of this in Job. 'And a parcel of wisdom fetches more than red coral.' Now, this species of coral is the type used for jewellery and, in its natural form, grows as a branched formation nearly always at considerable depth and never less than about eighty feet. There are many other references to coral, and in Ezekiel we read of the ships of Tarshish bringing back black coral from Edom.

But throughout the Bible there are continuing references to a commodity which the average reader would never relate with diving. And yet this commodity probably accounted for more underwater work in Bible times than all the pearls, corals and sponges put together. The reference in the Bible to which I refer to is that of the purple dye. In the Book of Exodus for example, there are the detailed instructions for the robing of the tabernacle. 'Moreover thou shalt make the tabernacle with ten curtains of fine twined linen and blue, purple and scarlet.' When the Temple was being rebuilt in Jerusalem, King Hiram of Tyre sent to King Solomon craftsmen who were skilled 'To work in gold and silver, in brass, in iron, in stone, in timber, in purple, in blue, in fine linen.' According to Josephus, Solomon's charioteers were dressed in tunics of purple.

Tekhelet, the Hebrew word for the purple dye, became associated with royalty, and it even took on a religious significance so that a thread of *Tekhelet* had to be included in every four-cornered garment. The purple *Tekhelet* dye was one of the most valuable commodities in the ancient world and according to Pliny could be compared in luxury to the pearl.

But what, one might ask, has this *Tekhelet* dye got to do with diving? The answer is that this dye was obtained, and indeed is still extracted, from the Murex shell, and particularly from the *Murex brandaris* and the *Murex trunculus*. To this very day, if you walk along any of the shores of Syria or Lebanon or northern Israel, you will come across the remains of hills of crumbled Murex shells that recall the dye factories that were part of a major industry along this coastline in Bible times.

Nowadays, in Italy, where the *Murex brandaris* is considered a delicacy, the shell is harvested by trawlers with specially designed dredgers. But the ancients had no such techniques and had to rely on the fisherman and the diver. Pliny has an account of the conventional fisherman's technique which involved the use of baskets filled with a species of snail to which the Murex was partial. These would be strung together on long ropes and lowered to the bottom of the sea. This was a slow process, and Murex recovered by these means could go nowhere near to satisfying the demands of the dye industry. In the early part of this century an Austrian chemist named Friedlander wanted to see how many shells would be required to produce a given quantity of dye. His experiments showed that for the production of just one and a half grams of dye no less than twelve thousand Murex shells were needed. There is no doubt, therefore, that a great proportion of Murex harvest in ancient times was collected by diving. In fact, Pliny himself confirms this when discussing alternative dyes and advocating the use of more easily obtained vegetable dyes which were, as a result, cheaper.

'Trans Alpine Gaul can produce vegetable dyes (like) Tyrenian oyster pearl just as well as it can other colours. To get these, nobody seeks the Murex oyster in the depths offering his person as bait to sea monsters while he hastens to snatch his booty and exploring a bottom that no anchor yet has touched, merely to discover the means for a matron to charm her paramour more easily and for a seducer to ensnare another's wife. There one stands on land to harvest dyes as we harvest crops; and though there is a complaint that the dye washes out with use, except for this defunct luxury could have bedecked himself in brighter colours and certainly with less risk to life.'

There is no doubt that diving for the Murex must have been one of the major industries in Bible times; but who were these divers and from where did they come? Certainly the majority of them must have been Phoenicians because they were the biblical men of the sea; but if we turn again to the Bible we find the following quotation which was known as the traditional blessing said to have been conferred on the Hebrew Tribe of Zebulun. 'For they sucked the affluence of the seas, the hidden treasures of the sand.' According to the *Talmud*, the traditional volumes of Jewish Law, this quotation referred to the

127

members of the tribe engaged in the gathering of the *Tekhelet*, namely, the Murex. In the later period of the New Testament the purple dye continued to be among the rarest of commodities. The woman called Lydia was 'A seller of purple'.

In the Roman world the purple continued to be the highest mark of distinction. In Rome, the Equities wore a narrow band of purple on their togas, whereas the Senators were distinguished by a single broad band of purple down the front of the tunic. The Imperator wore a purple cloak and a victorious General on his return to Rome would receive a purple cloak with gold embroidery. The dye factories of Tyre continued right into the late Roman period when the finest of all, the doubly dyed purple silk and wool, became more or less the prerogative of royalty, so that under the Roman emperors, any person outside the Court who wore a garment dyed with pure purple, could be convicted of treason and put to death.

Before I finish with the purple dye, I must tell of this parable in the *Talmud* which I find so appealing. 'Once we were travelling on board a ship and we saw a chest in which was set precious stones and pearls and it was surrounded with a species of fish called Karisa. A diver went down to bring up the chest but a fish noticed him and was about to wrench his thigh. Thereupon he poured upon it a skin bottle of vinegar and it sank. A divine voice came forth saying unto us, what have you to do with the chest of the wife of Rabbi Hanina son of Dosa who is to store in it purple blue for the righteous in the world to come.'

The Karisa was probably a shark and it seems to me that this must be one of the earliest references to a shark deterrent.

In continuing our search for the diver in the Bible we find the combat diver or swimmer, in fact the biblical frogman. In the Book of Kings we read, 'Now in the fourteenth year of Hezekiah did Sennacherib King of Assyria come up against all the fenced cities of Judah and took them.' One such siege is illustrated in the incredible Assyrian Palace reliefs in the British Museum. Dating from the 7th century BC, it shows a swimmer crossing a river and he is aided by an inflated animal bladder into which he is either sucking or blowing air. Some have suggested that this bladder is a primitive type of aqualung and that the soldier is actually swimming underwater, whereas others conclude that the bladders serve as a pair of water wings for the warrior, who was presumably a non-swimmer.

Whether the Assyrian frogman was swimming underwater or on the surface, is a matter of conjecture, but there is ample evidence that the naval frogman was common in antiquity and in Bible times. The Jewish Philosopher, Philo, who wrote in the 1st century AD, tells that the hours of darkness were the best for divers engaged in war operations. He goes on to suggest that they could be used to bore holes in the bottoms of enemy ships. Then there is the account that Aristotle gives of a certain skilled diver in nearby Greece called Scillias and his daughter Cyana, who were employed in the defence of Mount Pelios in the cutting of the anchor ropes of attacking Persian galleys. This same Scillias, as well as attacking enemy boats, was also engaged in the recovery of large quantities of treasure from the sunken Persian ships, and this is one of the first accounts that we have of a diver engaged in underwater salvage. These early treasure hunters were scoffed at by the 1st-century Roman poet, Manchius, who wrote, 'Others find pleasure in seeking the world beneath the sea and plunge into the waves trying to visit Mereus and sea nymphs; they carry off the booty of the ocean, taking possession of wrecked ships in the depths and greedily explore the sandy bottom of the sea.'

Earlier, I quoted a story from the Talmud, and there are others which are really quite revealing. One refers to the methods used by divers in the recovering of large heads of coral. This passage tells of coral diving in the Persian Gulf. The writer describes how a large boat was filled with sand until it sank to the bottom of the sea. 'Then a diver goes down, ties a rope of flax to the coral while the other end is tied to the ship and the sand is then taken and thrown overboard and as the boat rises it pulls up the coral with it.' The account goes on to relate that coral is worth twice its weight in silver and that there were three ports that traded in underwater produce; two of these belonged to the Romans and one to the Persians, the Romans dealing solely in coral and the Persians only in pearls.

There is another good story about divers in the Talmud; one told by

Rabbi Judah, the Indian. He says, 'Once we were travelling on board a ship when we saw a precious stone that was surrounded by a snake. A diver descended to bring it up. Thereupon the snake approached with the purpose of swallowing the ship when a raven came and bit off its head and the waters were turned into blood. A second snake came, took the head of the decapitated snake and attached it to the body and it revived. Again the snake approached intent on swallowing the ship. Again a bird came and severed its head. Thereupon the diver seized the precious stone and drew it into the ship. We had with us assorted birds. As soon as we put the stone upon them they took it up and flew away with it.' Elsewhere in the Talmud there is this very short cautionary tale. 'It once happened at Asia that a diver was lowered into the sea and only his leg was brought up.'

Any study of the history of underwater exploring in the Holy Land cannot be complete without the account of Alexander the Great's capture of Phoenician Tyre in 332 BC. As legend has it, this was achieved with the aid of Alexander's divers who had, prior to the attack, cut through the beach defences. The Emperor, hearing from his divers of the wonders of the deep, was determined to see for himself, but as he was a non-swimmer, he commissioned his shipwrights to build a diving bell. This early submersible and the account of Alexander's initiation into the deep, is given in an early Arab legend.

> 'A wooden case ten cubits long by five cubits wide. Windows of glass were set in it and the wood itself was treated with resin wax and other substances to keep out the salt water. Alexander and two of his secretaries, both skilled draftsmen, then entered the case after which he gave orders that it was to be closed up and the lid impregnated with the same substance to make it watertight. Two large ships then put out to sea. Iron weights of lead and stone had been fastened to the inside of the box to carry it down into the sea. Poles of wood were placed from one ship to another and the case was then suspended on this gantry. Afterwards the cables were played out and the case descended into the water.'

This story has been repeated often in much embroidered form in

130

Arab, Greek, Indian and mediaeval literature, and it was a favourite subject for illustration, many of which show the King surrounded by giant monsters of the deep.

I have written about men who, for various reasons during the biblical and post-biblical periods, dived to search the bottom of the sea. But there have been occasions when nature, in a convulsive mood, has caused the bottom of the sea itself to be revealed. If you walk along the shore of the Mediterranean looking at the various ancient sites, you cannot fail to notice the frequent signs of earthquakes, earth tremors and natural catastrophes. These were short violent moments that upset the delicate balance between sea and land, so that what was at one moment dry land had become sea, and where once the sea stood there is land. The coast of ancient Palestine is no exception, and history records many earthquakes and tidal waves that have struck this coast, often with catastrophic results.

During my research I came across the account of one such catastrophe that occurred on this shoreline in the year AD 868. It is a remarkably graphic account of a tidal wave which struck this coast in that year. The tidal wave was preceded by a great sea bed movement and a drop in the level of the sea, so that from the shore the sea appeared to recede for miles leaving the whole of the ocean bottom exposed. The author of this account was one Michael, who was the Patriarch of Antioch in the 12th century AD, and he ascribes this story to Dionysius of Tell-Mahre, a previous Patriarch of the 9th century AD. This is the account.

> 'Botrys, a city of Phoenicia, situated on the seashore, fell in this violent earthquake. The great mountain that dominated the city was broken, overthrown suddenly by the violence of the shock and a large part fell into the sea. It was thrown far out into the sea by the earthquake; it lodged there, and made a long barrier in front of the city; the sea was left inside. There remained an entrance towards the city so that there came into being a great miraculous harbour capable of holding large ships. When this terrible earthquake took

place at Beirut and in the other cities of the Phoenician coast the sea by the command of God drew back about two miles. The depth of the sea was revealed, and many things were seen there, including ships that had been wrecked, filled with their cargo. Instead of being frightened by these horrors, those on the shore hurried to take possession of these treasures hidden in the deep; they entered there and loaded them up to take back. Others hurried up to enter in their turn. Then the terrible power of the sea returned and overwhelmed them in its depths by the secret plan of God. Those who were still only on the shore seeing the sea return ran off to escape, but the earthquake threw the buildings down on them and they were buried. This happened at all the cities of the coast, and especially at Beirut where the fire took over after the destruction of the city; the fire lasted two months and the stones were consumed and turned to ashes. The Emperor Justinian sent much gold; men looked for the bodies of the victims to bury them and rebuilt part of the city.'

Earthquakes of this sort are fairly rare, but this account does serve to remind one that the continental shelves are an ever-changing terrain. The character of the sea bed changes with a far greater rapidity than its land counterpart. This can be caused by natural phenomena, or by an unnatural disturbance of seas' currents. For example, constructions of breakwaters or sea-dumping of waste material can result in the most extraordinary changes in sea contours for many miles from the original cause.

One of the dividends that the nautical archaeologist can derive from this is that it has been known for archaeological material suddenly, and for no immediately accountable reason, to reveal itself on the sea bed. An area which for years divers might have thought was archaeologically barren can suddenly prove to be rich with material. One such case occurred in the Carmel area, and I will tell of this in the next chapter.

X

Treasures of Asher

And the channels of the sea appeared.

II SAMUEL 22.16

After a recent talk, I was asked this question: 'Where do you think the most important underwater finds in the Bible Lands will be made in the future?' I replied that it was impossible to anticipate the importance of finds, because these were likely to turn up anywhere; but if I were to be asked which was the most lucrative area, then I would unhesitatingly choose that strip of coastline that stretches from Tyre to the north in Lebanon, to Caesarea to the south in Israel. This is near the region which, according to biblical tradition, was the country of the Tribe of Asher.

The main reason for my choice is that this was the area in which there has been more or less continuous maritime activity right back to pre-history times, although I must say that the undersea terrain here is not particularly conducive to the preservation of wrecked material. None the less, there is one short length of this coast of Asher in particular which has in recent years begun to acquire a reputation as an underwater archaeological treasure chest. This is the stretch of shoreline that extends from the base of Mount Carmel southwards to Athlit. If you stand on the top of Carmel on the spot where Elijah wrestled with the Priests of Baal, and look down, the area of sea immediately beneath you is the happy hunting ground for many an archaeological group, and also sadly for the less scrupulous treasure hunter.

Why this spot in particular? It is because the sea bed terrain along this stretch has, by a combination of geological and recent man-made causes, begun as it were to thin out, and the sand on the bottom is now giving rather less cover to buried material than is normal. The sandy beach which runs from the site of the ancient Tell Shikmona to Athlit is paralleled by a submerged limestone reef, less than a mile offshore, and, as a result, the sea bed that lies between the shore and the reef is, for its nine-mile length, shaped rather like a shallow pan. The reason for this thinning out is that the sand on the beaches has been found to be suitable for building use, and has, over the last few years, been commercially extracted. This, together with the construction of a new breakwater at the Chof ha Carmel bathing beach, has caused changes in the direction and force of the sea currents. The effect of all this has been to reduce the covering thickness of sand on the sea bed so that thinly obscured artefacts are less likely to escape the eye of the skilled searcher.

I hesitate to give the impression that historical material now lies scattered and visible on the sea bed just waiting to be picked up, but with the constant moving of the comparatively thin layers of sand in this shallow area, detection by eye becomes that much easier. However, it still needs the trained and accustomed eye to detect the slight aberration from nature that indicates the partially buried artefact. This talent is rarely possessed by one who is unaccustomed to underwater conditions, for just as urban man cannot match his rural cousin in understanding the ever-changing landscape, so it is rare for the eye accustomed only to the world above the sea readily to re-adjust to the quite different environment of the underwater world. It takes much diving and understanding of submerged terrain before you can begin to pick out the merest tell-tale clue from among the many shapes and colours of the sea bed in its natural form.

Occasionally, one comes across a diver who seems to have been born with this talent, and one such was Udi Galilee, the son of my old diving friend Yoske Galilee. Udi learnt to swim before he could walk and cannot remember a time when he did not accompany his father on snorkelling expeditions to their local Haifa beach.

Ever since my first visit to Israel, Yoske and I had corresponded off and on. Just before I was about to leave for a further visit, I received a letter in which he urged me to visit Haifa before I did anything else. He wrote, 'You always said that Udi has the eye of an eagle. Well come and see what he has found; you will not be sorry.'

A week later, with mask, snorkel and fins, the three of us threaded our way through the crowded beach at Shikmona and into the shallows. It was the Sabbath, and all of Haifa seemed to be there. We put on our equipment and I followed the two others into the waves expecting a fair swim before we reached our destination. But imagine my surprise when Udi stopped and turned at armpit height only about fifty feet from the shore, and called back, 'This is where I found it.'

I still did not know what 'it' was, for as Yoske put it, 'We are not telling you because we want you to experience the excitement that Udi felt when he made his discovery.' Yoske and his wife Carmella are two wonderful people whose kindness and hospitality know no limits and I had now become accustomed to Yoske's generosity of spirit. If it was his wish that I share their thrill of discovery to its limits, so be it, I would be patient.

'But what could you find here on a crowded beach in just four feet of water?' I asked. 'Aha,' replied Yoske. 'That is the point. Hundreds of people have been swimming and snorkelling here backwards and forwards every day for years, but it took the eye of the eagle, the eye of my Udi, to find it.'

My patience was beginning to come to an end. 'For God's sake, Udi, what did you find?' Yoske gave Udi a nod and, with a grin, Udi produced, from a small plastic bag that he had attached to his wrist, a bronze figurine. It was no more than four inches high and, as it lay in the palm of Udi's hand, I could see that it was of the Goddess of the Sea, Aphrodite. One foot was missing and the figure was corroded, and yet somehow it still retained much of its original form and grace. 'And that is not all, Alex,' said Yoske, adding, 'Show him, Udi.' The rest of the contents of the bag were revealed; three more bronze figurines, one which stood on its original pedestal.

The figurines went back into the bag and Udi, under Yoske's direction, took me on an underwater excursion explaining every so often, as we popped to the surface, how he made this find. 'It was very simple,' he said. 'I was snorkelling here one morning and I saw something just under the sand, so I picked it up. I brushed the sand off and found that it was this Venus, so I started looking around for more and then I found the three other figures.' On the way back to Yoske's flat, and to what I knew would be Carmella's gargantuan lunch, I heard the rest of the story.

Udi reported his find to the Undersea Exploration Society, and the next day about thirty volunteer divers were rounded up to continue the search. Starting off from the original spot, the snorkellers and divers scoured the shallows never more than six feet deep, and the fruits of their search proved more than any of them had imagined in their wildest dreams. Hundreds of small artefacts were recovered over a widespread area of about three hundred yards by fifty yards, and these included a large quantity of coins, a bronze steelyard, a superb bronze neck chain, fish hooks, a sewing needle, countless ship's rivets and a great number of pottery sherds.

This material was presented to the Haifa Maritime Museum and Avner Raban was given the job of studying this material. On a later occasion, I examined all the pieces with Avner in the Museum, and they are a most interesting, although puzzling, group. Puzzling because of the wide span of time represented by the material. Take the coins for example: there was the Roman group extending from AD 98 to 161, and then a Byzantine collection of thirty coins of various dates, seven from the time of Arcadius, being 395 to 408, minted in Constantinople, and one Theodora coin of 1055 to 1056.

Avner pointed out that this clearly indicated that this material must have come from wrecks of different periods which had all jumbled together in the comparatively shallow water. This was confirmed by the pottery which seemed to spread in age from the 2nd to the 5th century AD.

Further finds made at the time, but which bore no relation to the other material, were two copper bowls, a lead plummet, another lead plummet covered with copper and attached to a copper chain; and then an entirely separate hoard of coins consisting of no less than eighty-six pieces from the times of Antiochus the Eighth and Ninth, from the beginning of the 1st century BC. This hoard was found in hard silt of the sea bed in a small hole about one square yard in area. The Shikmona area has, to date, I suppose, yielded up thousands of copper nails, silver and gold coins of all periods, and even pieces of eight from the 17th century. The finds that I have mentioned were those that were brought into the Maritime Museum, but this can only be a small proportion of the finds that have been made either accidentally or by amateur or professional searchers.

I suppose that, in truth, the Shikmona Dish is a treasure-hunter's paradise and an archaeologist's nightmare. However, there are compensations, and one such revealed itself during a recent winter period when the tide remained exceptionally low. The remains of a Chalcolithic site was discovered at a depth of about nine feet. This was a site which had been originally on land, but had been overcome by the sea and the finds here included, among other things, a basalt censer, adzes, a fan-like flint scraper together with other stone tools, a fire altar in a perfect state of preservation containing some half-burned twigs, and then, as if to emphasise the confusion of the Shikmona site, a well-preserved keel of a small boat of the 3rd century AD.

About three years after my snorkelling trip with Yoske and Udi; I was in the Haifa Maritime Museum, when I bumped into Udi. He said that he often popped into the Museum to visit some of his old friends. 'Who are your old friends?' I enquired. He replied that these were all the pieces that he had discovered and given to the Museum, but in particular the Roman gods and goddesses. 'You remember the bronze figurines, don't you? My father and I showed you where we found them.' He took me over to where they now stood carefully cleaned and conserved and resplendent in their pristine case. I must say that I found the little Venus quite touching in her traditional pose which in later years came to be known by art historians as 'The Pose of Modesty'.

One of my diving colleagues on the Tanit figurine wreck at Shave Zion was Shelly Wachsmann, who at that time was studying at the Hebrew University in Jerusalem. Shelly's interest in underwater work has continued to this day and he is now the leader of the Israel Department of Antiquities and Museum's underwater team. It was in this capacity that he and a colleague, Kurt Raveh, headed the preliminary salvage excavation of yet another site from the treasure chest of Asher. In dating these discoveries, which were by far the most ancient yet found, Shelly estimated them to be of the latter part of the late Bronze Age or the early Iron Age. In Palestinian chronological periods this would correspond to somewhere between 1100 and 1300 BC, among the oldest material discovered to date in the eastern Mediterranean.

The site was near Kibbutz ha Hotrim, and Shelly described the artefacts as being scattered about on the hard clay sea bed in an area that had been temporarily swept clean of its sand by sea action. Here again we had another example of material more or less revealing itself temporarily in this area. The two archaeologists, assisted by volunteer divers from Kibbutz Nahsholim and divers from the Nature Reserve Authority first of all uncovered two exceptionally large stone anchors, and as they proceeded, hundreds of small metal artefacts and pottery sherds revealed themselves. The sherds for the most part were of a fairly late date, but Shelly was intrigued by the nature of the metal artefacts. These included horse bits, blades, chisels, small pieces of copper and bronze ingots, and even a plough-share. All of these metal objects were broken, and the impression was that they were being transported as scrap.

Shelly wrote to me shortly after his work on this site, and he expressed the view that although this excavation was still in its early stages, he had the impression that the material was part of the cargo of a ship, and he was struck by the resemblance between these cargo contents and those of the Cape Gelidonya Wreck, one of the oldest found to date. One passage of his letter, however, that particularly interested me was his report of finding a number of metal ingots, including one entire bun-shaped ingot. Some years ago a colleague from the British Sub-Aqua Club, Hume Wallace, brought me a copper bun ingot which he had found in Plymouth Sound. The ingot was semi-spherical in shape, about five inches in diameter, and closely resembled the sort of copper ingots which were the specialisation of Dr Beno Rothenberg with whom I had liaised for many years on the subject of the Island of Jezarit Fara'un.

Coincidentally, Rothenberg was in London at that time to open his Timna Exhibition at the British Museum which dealt with his major excavation in the South of Israel's Negev Desert. I took Hume's ingot along to the exhibition opening and showed it to Rothenberg who was accompanied by Dr R S Tylecote, the expert on ancient metallurgy. They were intrigued at the ingot's history and, on a subsequent analysis, Dr Tylecote confirmed that the ingot was almost certainly of Middle East Bronze Age origin. The stories of the Phoenicians who had sailed as far as Britain to barter for tin from Cornwall are well known. Is it possible that this ingot was evidence of this trading? Could the ingot have come from a wreck? We will never know, for when I told Hume Wallace of Dr Tylecote's conclusion, his pleasure was tinged with some regret. 'Do you know,' he sighed, 'professional divers had been picking up these things from Plymouth Sound for years to be melted down as scrap. Nobody knew what they were, and I think that this is probably about the last one.'

The treasures of Asher are popping up with increasing regularity and the most exciting by far is a discovery made by a graduate student of the University of Haifa, Yehoshua Ramon in November 1980. Elisha Linder, who was Ramon's professor at Haifa, wrote to me shortly after this discovery and his pen seemed to tremble with excitement. 'Ramon was snorkelling just for pleasure in shallow water at Athlit and discovered a bronze ram from a galley. It is the most amazing thing that I have ever seen from the sea and it's probably one of the most important discoveries ever made in the Mediterranean. My dear friend you must come soon and share in our joy.' The reaction of the marine archaeological world to this discovery is best illustrated by the words of the distinguished scholar, Lucien Basch. 'Ramon discovered a portion of an ancient warship; such a portion was beyond the wildest hope of any marine archaeologist because it was the bronze ram of a galley, the main offensive weapon of maritime warfare in the Mediterranean for the greater portion of post-Bronze Age antiquity – this weapon, however terrible, is also a thing of beauty.'

I thought of Basch's words as I stood in the basement of the Haifa Maritime Museum with Elisha and the Museum Director, Dr Joseph Ringel and saw for the first time this awe-inspiring weapon of antiquity. To understand the emotions that this artefact raises in all who see it, it is necessary to understand that the ram of the ancient warship has, until now, only been known through iconology on coins, pottery and sculpture. This legendary ram had been written about, talked and argued about for centuries and yet not one person had ever seen one. Its discovery is to marine archaeology what the Dead Sea Scrolls are to biblical archaeology. To those who have seen it, it seems to have the effect of either striking one dumb or elating one to the height of eloquence. On a subsequent occasion I was with Professor J Richard Steffy as he lectured to a group of international marine archaeologists on his interim examination of the ram. Steffy, a shipwright by training, is acknowledged as probably the foremost authority on ancient ship construction. 'Ladies and gentlemen, you are now looking at the ballistic missile of the ancient world.' This struck a note with those of us from Britain who had been reading of the effect of the Exocet missile in the Falklands conflict. In his report Steffy wrote, 'It is one thing to read about these ancient weapons and study their depictions on coins and reliefs, but quite another to actually see one. This ram is impressive, almost hypnotic at first glance. I had not expected so much beauty, technology and expertise to be lavished on an ancient warship.' And then about the timbers which attached the ram to the ship: 'Seldom have I seen such perfection in the fitting of seams and surfaces, or such discipline in the cutting of mortices.' One day, when its conservation treatment has been completed, the ram will be displayed for all to see.

In his report, Steffy wrote of the timbers to the ram, 'If these few preserved timbers are indicative of the manner in which ancients built their warships, what a treat it would be to find such a hull intact.' Of course, everyone who sees the ram inevitably poses the question – but where is the ship? Where, indeed? For the divers of the Centre for Maritime Studies have searched in vain. But I have no doubt that one day the constantly moving sands of Asher will reveal something of that ancient warship to the inevitable excitement of the archaeological world.

There is a sad postscript to this story. The discoverer of the ram, Yehoshua Ramon, died from cancer just one year later.

XI

Red Sea Wreck

Came they into the wilderness of Sinai.

EXODUS 19.1

If Mecca is the ultimate place of pilgrimage for all those who follow the Prophet Muhammed, then Ras Muhammed might justly claim to be the Mecca of all divers. Situated at the southernmost tip of the Sinai Desert where the Gulf of Aqaba meets the Gulf of Suez, Ras Muhammed, with its Bay of Marsa Bareka and nearby Sharm el-Sheikh, has been the ultimate destination of thousands of divers who, over the last few years, have made their pilgrimage starting at Eilat, diving the various and varied sites as they travel south along the eastern shores of the Sinai Desert.

I first came here late in 1968 at the termination of our Jezirat Fara'un expedition of that year. We had heard that two soldiers, having spent a rest-day snorkelling, had come across a quantity of pottery on the sea bed. They reported this find to their local military commander, who in turn sent a message up to Eilat. The Eilat authorities, knowing that there were members of the Undersea Exploration Society of Israel diving with us, passed this information on to Yoske Galilee, and having a couple of days to spare before I caught my plane, I accepted Yoske's invitation to join their party down to Sharm. The site that we were taken to by one of the soldiers was about a hundred yards offshore, at a depth of twenty-five feet. The bottom was flat and sandy and here and there, sticking out of the sand, we could see small pots about twelve inches high. They were of decorated pottery and had an Islamic look about them. Scraping some of the sand away, further pottery immediately became visible, and as we worked with our hands and with trowels that we had brought with us, it became quite obvious that this was a considerable find.

We returned to the beach for a rest and midday snack, and in the afternoon returned to the site with one objective in mind. Yoske and I, together with the others, had discussed the possibility of the site marking a wreck, and by the position of the pottery there was every indication that this would not be difficult to find. This was to be the case, because within only twenty minutes or so, the first signs of timber became evident, and we knew that we had a ship beneath us. There was not much point in continuing with our search because we were quite satisfied that a wreck existed here, and besides, with the few hours left, a dive at Ras Muhammed was a must. Those few who had dived at this legendary spot, had reported that there was nothing like it in the whole of the Red Sea, and within the hour we were finding this to be incredibly true. I had never seen water of such unbelievable clarity, coral of such abundance and size, and fish in so many numbers. But above all, there were the sharks: large, graceful and majestic creatures. We were careful to keep close together, for this was the sharks' domain and we were the visitors. Every now and then a twelve-foot, white-tipped predator would come in from the distant blue, glide past us with the odd flick of his large tail, and with a cursory glance, fin off.

Except for their few inspections, the sharks did not seem to be very interested in us, and we were left to enjoy our dive to its full. The next morning we returned once again for an early dive in this wondrous

143

place, and I was rewarded on this occasion by the sighting of a Manta Ray, an enormous, yet gentle and graceful, creature.

But the main object of this visit had been to look at the Sharm el Sheikh wreck as we now knew it to be, and Yoske was excited at the prospect of arranging an expedition as soon as possible. Arrangements were made for this to take place in April of the following year, and Yoske asked me if I would like to join the Israeli Group. I knew that my commitments for that time were such that I could not possibly spare the time, and, sadly I declined. But as luck would have it, at very short notice in April, I was asked to fly to Cyprus to investigate a prospective architectural development with a client. Of course, I could not resist the temptation, and at the close of my Cyprus business, I calculated that three days would be good enough for a flying visit to the Sharm el Sheikh site which I knew was now in full swing. I dropped in unannounced to a delighted Yoske, who was the expedition's photographer, and Avner Raban who was leading the expedition. I had arrived at the right time to see that the whole site was in the course of excavation, revealing a large wooden boat which had split open and had now become totally flattened. The whole area was covered with a metal grid for surveying purposes, groups of divers were carefully measuring within their own areas, a photographer's tower was in position for the taking of stereoscopic photographs, and two large air lifts were working away at full pressure. In the extreme clarity of these waters, the whole operation could be taken in at one go, and I remember thinking at the time how envious British archaeological divers would be if they could see such perfect working conditions.

Avner told me that, as the wreck was not too far from the shore, it was decided to supply air to the divers directly from a beach-located compressor, and more or less to do away entirely with the use of compressed air bottles. The air-lifting equipment was placed on a raft above the wreck, and a second raft held a water pump to supply pressurised water to cleaning hoses. As there was almost no sea current, the residue of sand from the air-lift tended to remain static, thereby reducing the visibility and so water hoses were used as a means of creating an artificial current which carried the air-lifted sand away from the site.

It appeared that the wreck itself had been separated from the sea bottom sand by a hard crust of coral just a few inches thick, which had the effect of encasing the remains of the ship entirely, and insulating the timbers from a normal decaying process. Avner told me that the first thing which became apparent when the coral crust was removed, was that the ship had foundered as a result of fire: this had destroyed all the construction above the water line, including the bridge and masts, and the fire appeared to have been extinguished only as the sea entered the ship's hold. He said that the vessel probably sank soon after the fire, and he therefore assumed that it was at anchor, and it was likely that the crew succeeded in reaching the shore, taking their personal belongings with them. Avner supported this theory on the basis that no small items or coins were found.

The part of the ship that remained was mostly on the port side, consisting of a large portion of the keel, many ribs and a considerable amount of planking. One item of interest that was found in the middle of the wreck, was the base of a clay oven. Beside this, in an upturned position, was the wooden roof of the cabin, and both in front and behind the cabin, were found two large pottery jars, each with a capacity of about thirty litres. These jars were fixed firmly between timber ribs, and their bases consolidated in a mixture of burnt clay and tar. Close by were many fragments of crude pottery, glazed bowls and dishes, and also pieces of a small, Chinese porcelain bowl.

Although the ship itself, of which I will have a little more to say later, was of real interest, what I found quite fascinating was the vast amount of pottery which lay between the ribs, mostly on the port side. A great deal of this pottery had already been removed, and was in the expedition's store. As I was to learn subsequently, this pottery cargo had consisted of almost one thousand pottery flasks. These flasks were unglazed and decorated on the exterior with a combination of incised geometric patterns and mouldings. All of the flasks had a clay sieve at the base of the neck, similar to perforated sieves that one comes across in water jugs from Egypt. Most of the flasks had lids of a cupola design, and many of these lids were themselves perforated.

I was only able to stay one day with the Sharm el Sheikh expedition, for I desperately wanted to get in a day's surveying at Jezirat Fara'un in order to add to the information that was now planning itself out on my drawing board. I was then to spend a day after that in Jerusalem to meet with some of my archaeologist friends, before returning to England. However, the following year I was able to get together with Avner, who had completed much of his research on the Sharm wreck, and this is what he told me.

Regarding the ship itself, wood samples from the keel were examined in the laboratory, and showed that the vessel had been constructed of a species of fir common in the northern Mediterranean countries, or Europe. But by its construction the ship indicated possibly a Turkish or eastern Mediterranean origin. Avner, however, was, as I had anticipated, particularly intrigued by the pottery, for much to his surprise he could find no comparative material elsewhere. Even the purpose for which the flasks were intended has still remained a matter for speculation. He pointed out that the sieve and the cover were probably designed to prevent pollution by insects or other impurities, but it was also noted that the pottery was porous and this might have been deliberate so as to ensure cooling by evaporation.

However, Avner was puzzled as to why such a large cargo of fragile and fairly inferior quality pottery was carried as merchandise on an ocean-going ship. He pointed out that one might expect a vessel of this sort along the Nile and on the large rivers of Arab countries, but what was this sort of vessel doing in the Red Sea, the shores of which were inhabited almost exclusively by the Bedouin? He conjectured, therefore, that the flasks might possibly have served as containers for drugs such as hashish or opium, or for spices such as cinnamon and cloves. Following up this line of research he consulted with experts in the Drug Laboratory of the Israeli Police, but they rejected the possibility of the vessels having been used to contain drugs as, they claimed, hashish had never been known to be transported in pottery vessels of this type, and that no traces had been found in the jars themselves.

I was given one of these small flasks, and it is still in my cabinet together with my other mementoes in my home. I have a rather fanciful idea about these flasks. I think that they might have been used for keeping small pieces of confectionery cool – possibly something like Turkish Delight. The confectionery, placed in the neck of the jar, would be kept cool by the evaporation of the water in the lower and main compartment of the vessel. I carried out a test to prove my theory, and on a warm summer day filled my jar with water, placed it in the sun, and then put some pieces of Turkish Delight and marshmallow in the neck, and I am pleased to say that after half an hour they had remained deliciously cool. In the absence therefore of any more acceptable theory, I submit that the Sharm cargo of nearly a thousand porous jars, was probably intended for the scented garden of some eastern sheikh for the delight, no doubt, of the ladies of the harem.

As for the dating of the wreck; well, as we know, there were no coins to assist in this and the pottery jars have not helped much. But, as Avner pointed out, the small pieces of Chinese porcelain were a great help in this direction. These pieces were submitted to R J Charleston of the Department of Ceramics of the Victoria and Albert Museum in London. Mr Charleston says that this porcelain is Late K'ang Hsi dating from the early years of the 18th century. In his view, the porcelain would not have ante-dated 1730 and this evidence, coupled with Avner's assessment of the ship's construction, brings him to a date somewhere around the second quarter of the 18th century.

The Sharm wreck itself was fully surveyed and then covered up, and samples of the pottery can now be seen in various of the Israeli museums. As far as I am aware, this wreck at Sharm is the only old wreck which has as yet been discovered and archaeologically recorded and excavated in this area of the Red Sea. But the potential for marine archaeology in the Red Sea must be limitless when one considers the ancient traditions of seafaring in this area, with the legendary routes from Africa to the Arabian States, and then on to China and the East. The young, adventurous and aspiring marine archaeologist might be well advised to follow the routes of Sinbad or of Vasco da Gama.

XII

Journeys with Mask and Snorkel

These see the works of the Lord, and his wonders in the deep.

PSALM 107.24

Looking back over the last twenty years, it would seem as if I have been on one continuous journey. As with most journeys, there were highlights and times when one halted and stayed a while, and it is these sojourns that have filled the earlier chapters. But often there was the short stop during which I had time only to taste very briefly of a location.

In travelling through the Bible Seas with mask, snorkel and fins, there were so many of these places that attracted me either because of their historical tradition or the evidence of something intriguing in the surf. A day or so walking the shores, snorkelling in the shallows and recording in my sketch pad, was the most pleasant of occupations and my sketchbooks are full of jottings and memories of these places. In reading through them again, I am reminded not only of glorious days in the sun, but also of the vast amount of archaeological material which still remains to be studied, and of those ancient sunken wrecks which undoubtedly lie hidden beneath the sands and are yet to be discovered.

Earlier in this book I alluded somewhat light-heartedly to our work being categorised as biblical marine archaeology, and I thought of this again when I came across the aims of the Palestine Exploration Fund at its foundation in 1865: 'Accurate and systematic investigation of the archaeology, topography, the geology and physical geography, the manners and customs of the Holy Land for biblical illustration.' I think that we have made some contribution to these aims by, for example, our seasons at Caesarea, Shave Zion and Jezirat Fara'un. But what of those areas that yet remain to be explored?

For example, what about Dor which lies on the Mediterranean beside the deserted village of Tantura, more or less halfway between Caesarea and Haifa? Here, the beach, for about half a mile, is strewn with constructions, a great many of which appear to be associated with maritime activity. Some years ago, Avner Raban and I spent a day from dawn to dusk exploring the remains of this ancient Canaanite city. We came across stone slipways which, judging by their dimensions, must have served large ships. There were berths cut into the rock and shallow rectangular basins. My first impulse was to interpret these basins as fishtanks, but I now doubt this. I suspect that these tanks, which in some cases were nothing more than pans, are relics of the purple dye industry which originated on this coastline.

In terms of coastal archaeology, this mile-length of shore compares for interest with any other in the Levant. Yet, except for cursory observations, the coast at Dor remains untouched. One day I hope that some enterprising institution will devote itself to the beaches of Dor, for I am convinced that here lies the key to much of the ancient maritime world of which we still know little.

Then there is the northernmost part of Israel's Mediterranean coastline at the rocky border with Lebanon. Achziv is mentioned in the Bible as one of the Canaanite cities that the Tribe of Asher failed to inherit. It was captured by Sennacherib, together with Acre and Sidon in 701 BC, and the Romans called it Ecdippe. All this I learned from

Elli Avivi, a bronzed, bearded, middle-aged resident who, convinced that the Government cared little for this area, unilaterally proclaimed himself the provisional head of the Independent State of Achziv. Just above the ancient harbour, in an old Arab house, Elli had established his residence of two sparsely furnished rooms, and a 'Museum' in which, lovingly displayed, were local crafts, the odd sherd or two and a fair amount of driftwood. For a modest entrance fee, the visitor enjoyed not only the contents of the Museum, but also a potted history of the area.

I was drawn to Elli and his attractive wife – who would not be? This couple loved the place for what it was, and they had committed themselves to protect its traditions as well as they were able. When I told Elli of my particular interest, he embraced me as a kindred spirit and promptly took me on an hour's tour of his rocky domain, pointing out many rock-cut features very similar to those that I had seen at Dor, and then the unmistakable remains of the ancient Harbour of Achziv.

The two southern ancient harbour cities of Ashdod and Ashkelon have been studied only in passing by marine archaeologists, although the land sites are very well documented. However, investigations at Ashkelon have been somewhat inhibited by the construction of a major new port, and I suppose that with so much to choose from, it is understandable that this area is going to be a long way down the list. Naturally, the most lucrative areas on the Mediterranean coast must be those on which ancient ports were located, and none is richer in legend than the port of Jaffa, known in antiquity as Yafo, meaning beautiful. This ancient coastal city is known in Greek mythology as the location of the Andromeda legend, where the Princess Andromeda was chained to a rock as a sacrifice to appease a sea monster, and she was rescued by Perseus on his winged horse, who slew the monster. Despite the fact that Jaffa is one of the oldest sea ports in the world, it still awaits a marine archaeological investigation.

A few miles north of Jaffa lie the coastal ruins of Appolonia, also known as Arsuf. History records this place as having been in ruins in 57 BC when it was rebuilt by the Romans. However, what attracted me here was not its biblical association, but guidebook references to a Crusader port and extensive mediaeval remains which I glimpsed when I first passed the site travelling along the coastal road. The opportunity for a day's trip occurred while I was visiting my son at Kibbutz Maagan Michael.

What an evocative spot Appolonia is. The mediaeval fortress sits atop a high cliff commanding distant views over both sea and land, though great portions of its battlements have slipped down some fifty feet or so to where they now lie, incongruously on the sandy beach.

Lieutenant Kitchener of the Royal Engineers, later to become Lord Kitchener, was a member of the Western Palestine Survey team, and in 1877 he wrote about Appolonia. 'The harbour is well constructed and measures three hundred feet from north to south and a hundred feet from east to west with an entrance barely thirty feet wide.' I found Kitchener accurate in his measurements, although search as I may I could not discover the thirty foot entrance. To me it appeared that the well constructed mediaeval harbour was entirely enclosed and not a harbour at all. My impression is that what remain in the shallows are in fact the footings of a large building. Certainly there is a finely built jetty with an intriguing fish-tail shaped end to it, and this would have served admirably as an unprotected quay. Locally there are stories of swimmers having spotted columns and capitals on the sea bed, although this, as far as I know, has never been verified. Here again is an unrecorded site for the enterprising diver.

But if we are to talk of mediaeval ports, then my choice of the most impressive is that at Athlit. In architectural terms alone, the Crusader remains of the Castle of the Pilgrims are magnificent. The Citadel was built by the Order of the Templars in the year 1218. They manned this coastal fortress for the whole of its seventy-three years existence and, although it was frequently attacked, it held out until the collapse of the Latin Kingdom in 1291. In fact, the departure of the Templar Knights from Pilgrims Castle to Cyprus, was the last act in the final fall of the Crusades. In 1337 the castle suffered from an earthquake and then much of it was dismantled for the rebuilding of Acre. In spite of this, the citadel, as it stands today, evokes – more than any other Middle East Crusader castle that I have visited – something of the spirit of those days when the Holy Land was the Frankish Kingdom.

Most of the sites that I am writing about in this chapter are those which are more or less virgin in marine archaeological terms, but Athlit is the one exception, for this is a site which has been very closely investigated by Elisha Linder, and my only connection was a day's stimulating visit with Joseph Shaw when Elisha explained the site to us.

A few years later, however, I was taken to dive on the wreck outside Athlit which had been dubbed 'The Flying Saucer Wreck'. I readily understood how this odd title came about when I dived down on to this thirty-foot-deep wreck. What I saw was a cargo of circular millstones; there were about sixty in all, and Elisha told me that a commercial barge with a derrick had been used to lift one of these which turned out to weigh nearly six hundredweight.

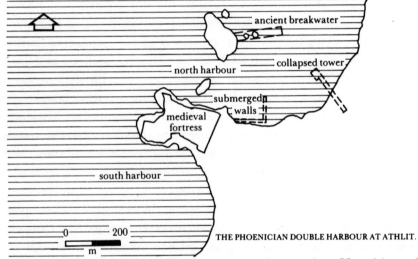

THE PHOENICIAN DOUBLE HARBOUR AT ATHLIT.

Elisha's story of his investigations is most interesting. He told us of the work carried out in the 1930s by C N Johns who was then the Director of the Department of Antiquities in Palestine. Although Johns' initial work was on the mediaeval castle, he was soon diverted to evidence of burials of the Canaanite period dating back to the 7th century BC. But what was particularly interesting from the maritime point of view, was just the geography of the place itself, because if there was ever a site for an ancient anchorage and harbour, then this was it. The site consists of a promontory which has on its north two small rocky islands within a natural bay, and on its south there is a further bay. This sort of promontory with a double bay has traditionally been

152

the sort of site which the ancient mariner would have used, for with a storm from the south, the north bay would be protected, and vice versa.

The three of us swam and snorkelled in the two bays and everywhere we saw signs of maritime construction. But the problem that Elisha had to unravel was identifying these structures with a specific period. Joe and I agreed with Elisha's thesis that with Canaanite material already having been found on land, coupled with the natural anchorage formations, the discovery of Canaanite construction was only a matter of time. Indeed, Elisha had already identified certain walls, some of which were on the beach and others slightly submerged, which had all the characteristics of Canaanite construction.

Elisha continued his work on the Athlit site for a few more years, and I was able to assist him in his investigations by obtaining from the British Ministry of Defence some aerial photographs of Athlit that had been taken by the Royal Air Force in the thirties. These photographs showed interesting shapes below the sea surface which related very closely with the other walls which Elisha had located. Concentrating on this area, his divers commenced to progress from a wall on the beach of the north bay which was composed of large rectangular-shaped stone blocks laid in a header fashion. At right angles to this wall the divers located a breakwater extending northwards into the sea. This break-water was formed by two parallel rows of well-preserved stone blocks, and the space between these walls had been filled with rubble and small rough stonework, so that the total width of the breakwater was about thirty feet. The structure was measured as three hundred feet long. At the very end, the divers discovered the remains of a collapsed tower.

Spurred on by this discovery, Elisha continued with his survey both on the mainland and on the islands, locating further marine walls and yet another breakwater some three hundred and fifty feet long and exactly the same construction as the previous one.

The final conclusion of the Athlit survey is argued convincingly by Elisha when he says that the breakwater remains are Late Phoenician and resemble very closely the late Iron Age maritime walls found at Tyre in Lebanon, corresponding to the 7th and 8th centuries BC.

Some time ago, I gave a talk to an Archaeological Society which covered, in a very compressed way, the scope of our work in Israel. One questioner asked why I had made no mention of the Sea of Galilee. A very reasonable question of course, because the Sea of Galilee and its tributary the River Jordan, have played a greater part in Christian tradition than any other stretch of water. I replied to the lady who asked this question that I had not touched on the Sea of Galilee solely because, to date, hardly any underwater or shore work has been carried out in this area at all. The reason is not difficult to find; it is because the development of marine archaeology in Israel has followed very much the Mediterranean and northern waters tradition, when specialists have tended to concentrate on the oceans rather than on inland seas, the former being assumed to be more fruitful. But in recent years, divers and archaeologists have begun to develop their interest in inland waters, in lakes and lochs and, to the surprise of many, have begun to produce archaeological material of great interest. For example, there are the Cranochs, the prehistoric defensive dwellings in the Scottish lochs, and the Neolithic lake settlements in Switzerland.

One day I am sure that the Sea of Galilee will be the site of some stimulating underwater research, but until then all that we can do is to recall some minor excursions. Edwin Link of whom I have written previously at Caesarea, came to the Sea of Galilee for a few days, and using the *Reef Diver*, a very much smaller version of his ocean-going *Sea Diver*, explored the sea bed at Magdala, the traditional site of the home of Mary Magdalen. Here he found, at a depth of about fifty feet below the surface of the lake, a strip of paving about thirty feet wide and no less than three hundred feet long. This paving was eighty feet offshore, with which it ran parallel. The road, for this is what we must assume it to be, was constructed of a cement base, mixed with small stones, and the top surface was set with cobblestones of various sizes, whose upper surfaces had been smoothed flat. From the evidence of this road, Link had surmised that the lake must have been considerably lower in Roman times than it is now, but this is an assumption which is certainly not borne out elsewhere around the shore. My guess is that we have here an example of a very local submergence, caused possibly by earthquakes which are not uncommon in this area. What interests me very much about Link's discovery is that if this road might be said to mark the edge of the lake in Roman times, when the eighty feet between the existing shoreline and the road is a submerged land site, and therefore one which could reveal much to us.

Ed Link did tell me of one other interesting find on Galilee which came about quite by accident. He said that he was heading down the lake, when *Reef Diver* developed engine trouble. While waiting for help to arrive, two of the occupants went in for a dive and immediately came across the rims of two bowls protruding above the mud on the bottom. These proved to be two complete Roman cooking pots dating from about the 1st century AD. Ed decided to work the area with a small air-lift, and finally recovered a further seven similar cooking pots, together with twenty-three other pottery vessels. These were all Roman of *terra cigelata* ware and excellent examples of their kind. In the same area as the pottery, two small stone anchors and a large quantity of sherds were found indicating, possibly, the presence of a wreck.

Link's discoveries are sufficient to show that there must be a great deal of material, particularly of the Roman period, at the bottom of the Sea of Galilee, and if Josephus is anything to go by, the whole of the Hebrews' Galilean Fleet lies there. In his *War of the Jews*, Josephus gives a short yet graphic account of the destruction of this fleet by the superior Roman forces.

My own, lone, brief expedition to the Sea of Galilee was a trip which I remember with increasing nostalgia. I had explained to Yochai ben Nun that I was on my way to Tiberius, from where I was planning to start a short boat and shore trip around parts of the Sea of Galilee. 'If you want a boat and some fishermen to take you, go to Avraham Tukerman and tell him that I sent you.'

One is never alone on a bus journey in Israel, and within a short time I was in intimate conversation with a little grey-haired, chubby lady who had the traces of a Brooklyn accent, and the appearance of an archetypal Yiddish momma. As it was, she turned out to be a senior obstetrician, and was going to Tiberius to give a series of lectures. This country never fails to surprise. As we entered the valley that overlooks Tiberius, we could see the snow-capped Mount Hermon in the distance and beneath us lay the blue expanse of the Sea of Galilee. Getting off at the bus station, I bid my comfortable companion 'shalom' and enquired the whereabouts of Avraham Tukerman's shop. I was directed through the narrow streets of the old town down towards the waterfront, where, as my guide had said, 'You cannot miss it.' True, for the shop, though more like a warehouse, was full of fishermen's baskets, wooden boxes and crates of crushed ice. There was a large, white marble counter surmounted by a vast pair of scales, behind which stood two giant refrigerators which spanned from floor to ceiling.

LAKE KINNERET (THE SEA OF GALILEE).

In the corner sat a small group of men crouched around a large, shallow pan from which there came the most delicious smell of simmering fish.

'Is Mr Tukerman here, please? I have been sent by Yochai ben Nun.' At the mention of that name one of the men turned his head sharply, stood up and came towards me with his arms outstretched. Grasping my hand in his, with the other on my shoulder, he looked at me enquiringly and asked, 'You know Yochai?' 'Yes,' I replied. 'Yochai suggested that I contacted you when I arrived in Tiberius.' 'If you are a friend of Yochai, you are my friend. Have you eaten?' he asked. I shook

156

my head. 'Come, we are just about to start.' And he led me towards the seated group and the simmering, pungent dish.

It was a meal that I will long remember. We all ate from the same dish. One broke a piece of pitta bread, opened it so as to grasp a piece of the white fish from the pan, and scooped it up, with a liberal soaking of gravy, into one's mouth. Each mouthful was followed by wiping the lips with a white paper napkin, and a sip of white wine.

'I can see you like our way of eating,' laughed Avraham. 'This is the way Yochai always liked to eat with me. We eat like fishermen; Yochai liked this way and I see you like this way as well.'

My sudden arrival had evoked in Avraham memories of his youthful days when he had served with Yochai ben Nun in the embryonic Israeli Navy. Yochai, who had become the Navy's first Commander, was a national hero whose exploits were legendary. Whoever I met who had known Yochai in those days never failed to come up with a story or two.

Avraham himself was a man of no mean stature. He was a native-born Israeli; a 'Sabra' of Moroccan parents. He told me that his father and all his forebears had been fishermen, but that now in his later middle-age he had been able to build up a business which no longer needed him to do the actual fishing, and he was, as he asked me, 'A wholesaler, yes?' After I explained to him my plan of wanting to go to various places around the Lake, he took me to two fishermen who ran a boat, arranged a very satisfactory hire charge, saying, 'You go where you like; you tell them, they go; you look and they fish.' It all sounded a sensible arrangement and the deal was done for me to start on the following morning.

My interest in Galilee really started with me reading *The Rob Roy on the Jordan* by John MacGregor. MacGregor was an itinerant canoeist who, having travelled the rivers and lakes of northern Europe and North America, decided, in 1852, to paddle his canoe *The Rob Roy* from the source of the River Jordan into the Sea of Galilee and around its shores. MacGregor was a rare enough Victorian explorer, for few of his contemporaries during the 19th century had any interest in the seas of the Holy Land. But not only was MacGregor interested in the Sea of Galilee and its geography, but also in what lay beneath the surface, and his pages are, as it were, splashed with observations on submerged stonework and indications of ancient marine constructions. Inevitably, I felt myself identifying with MacGregor and I could not help musing that if he had lived today, he would certainly be doing what I was attempting.

There was another tenuous connection which we had; it was that, when he was on his Bible Land expedition, he happened to be the Captain of the Canoe Club, and the Commodore of the Canoe Club at that time, to whom MacGregor dedicated his book, was His Royal Highness the Prince Albert, the Consort of Queen Victoria. My own trip to the Sea of Galilee coincided with the period when I was the Chairman of the British Sub-Aqua Club, during which time the President of the British Sub-Aqua Club was His Royal Highness the Prince Philip, Consort to Her Majesty Queen Elizabeth.

MacGregor's book is a delight; a combination of quite serious observation, *Boys Own Paper* type of adventure and pithy, 19th-century comment. The book is illustrated with MacGregor's own drawings, and I was happily given permission to examine MacGregor's original diaries and colourful sketches which are now housed in the Palestine Exploration Fund's archives.

My plan in the few days at my disposal was to see if I could follow in the wake of *The Rob Roy* for part of its journey, and to see whether it was possible to relocate some of the submerged material which MacGregor had pinpointed. The first thing I was to discover was that the Sea of Galilee was now no longer the clear limpid lake on which MacGregor had paddled over one hundred years ago. Pollution has sadly come here as it has throughout many of the seas of the world, and I was to find that the visibility was from average to poor. In spite of this, however, I was able to identify many of MacGregor's sites and in some cases the precise spots.

Our author had quite a lot to say about Tabgha on the west coast of the lake. Here I found as he had described; the warm rivulets of volcanic spring water which exuded from between the rocks on the beach and warmed the surface of the lake. But although MacGregor, who was usually very perceptive in these matters, had noticed the many rock features which broke the surface, he did not interpret these as I did. Encouraged by the pleasant temperature of the water, I spent an hour or so snorkelling among these rocks, and have concluded that the small Tabgha Bay was formed into a harbour by a semi-circular breakwater of which these rocks are the remnants.

At Koursy on the east side of the lake, MacGregor writes of having seen 'heavy rubble masonry of which part has fallen into deep water'. Later he comments, 'A few cut stones are submerged but no other remains of interest are to be seen, for the pile of large stones at the next point seem to be not artificial after I had examined them closely.' Here again I find myself at variance with my 19th-century predecessor; for had he had the means of diving he would have seen, just below the surface, a breakwater of carefully coursed stone blocks indicating certainly a harbour or, at the very least, a substantial quay. Koursy is widely accepted as the site of Gergesa, where the Gadarene Swine were drowned.

I was less successful in following the wake of *The Rob Roy* at Capurnaum. Now this is near the 4th-century AD synagogue, the site of the earliest synagogue at which Jesus was thought to have preached. I asked my boatman to drop me off about a hundred yards south of the landing stage leading to the synagogue, as I wished to examine the shoreline in this area. After arranging to be picked up at the landing stage an hour later, the boatman departed and I started my inspection. Intent on taking the dimensions of the base of the shoreline wall, I did not at first think that the violent, distant voice was directed at me. But on looking up I was astonished to see the brown-clad figure of a Franciscan monk bearing down on me shouting at the top of his voice with arms flailing. I was taken aback at this onslaught, and quite confused by this unprovoked aggression. I could not understand his Hebrew, at least I think it was Hebrew, and mumbled back hesitatingly in English. The voice that came back to me was in immaculate Germanic English – 'Vot you do here? Get off. Get off. Dis is verboten land?' I could not help it, I started to laugh, which made the friar even more angry. His face got redder and redder and he began to splutter and stamp. I tried to explain my presence but to no avail, so I thought it better to go meekly, and permitted my aggressor to march me off to the gate of the monastery, where I was handed over to a policeman whose

English was even poorer than my Hebrew, and who clearly thought it prudent to take me in his jeep to the police station.

The understanding sergeant, who, fortuitously, turned out to be an amateur skin diver, explained to me that I had trespassed on private land and, having telephoned the monastery to convey my apologies, I was then returned in the police jeep to the landing stage just in time to meet my boatman. So much for my survey of the Capurnaum beach.

When we arrived back at the small Tiberius fishing port, I was intrigued to see a wet-suited diver unloading a quite considerable fishing catch from his inflatable. I assumed that the fish had been caught with a spear, but I was soon corrected by the diver. He told me that he did not like using a spear gun and, in any case, this was not practical in the poor visibility. Instead he had evolved his own system of underwater fishing. 'This is what I do,' he said. 'I take with me in my left hand, this torch, and in my right hand this special pincher which I have invented.' His pincher operated on a scissors principle and looked very much like a tool for punching holes in leather, except that it was much longer.

The fisherman continued, 'I dive carefully to the bottom where I know the fish are. I give a few pieces of meat for the fish to eat and then I wait quietly. When the fish comes near I suddenly switch my torch on in his face; the fish goes, "Oh!" and straight away I pinch him with my pincher and put him straight in my bag.'

I could not help wondering, as I walked back into Tiberius, what the Galilee fishermen of the Bible would have made of the diving fisherman of today, with his catch of St Peter's fish.

XIII

Epilogue

Archaeology is digging up, not things, but people.

The adage quoted above was originated by one of my mentors, Sir Mortimer Wheeler, and it was one that he never tired of repeating. It is a view that I followed instinctively, for any discovery with which I have been associated has only come to life when I have been able to relate it to people and their time in history. It might be the peoples of The Bible, the Crusaders and their Arab foes or the Roman 'fishponders'. There have been the odd occasions when I have been able to identify a discovery with an individual person, or with a specific moment in history; sometimes both together, such as Sir Sidney Smith's block-ship and the Siege of Acre. As far as I am concerned, archaeology and history are intertwined, and it is the interaction between these two subjects that makes my adrenalin rise and gives me so much pleasure.

Nautical archaeology is the perfect study for those who share this motivation; for the discovery of a sunken wreck can only be compared with a Pompeii, for both tell of a single moment of catastrophe. In one case the sudden engulfing of a city by volcanic ash, and in the other the sinking of a ship with its cargo and crew. In both cases, sudden death and pitiful tragedy: but for the archaeologist it is the discovery of a moment in the past which has become frozen in time.

As a diver, I naturally look forward with anticipation to the prospects of future underwater discoveries. This area of nautical archaeology is a product of modern technology and requires high skills, and is accompanied on occasions with some element of risk. Perversely, it is the maritime-orientated underwater archaeologist who has, by his amphibious nature, done much to develop the study of shoreline archaeology.

The seashore is an area that has been almost totally overlooked by the land archaeologist. I suppose that one of the reasons for this neglect is the difficulty, indeed the impossibility, of excavating stratigraphically in water-logged sand. In common with other nautical archaeologists, I was surprised to find that the many shoreline structures, buildings and installations that I came across from time to time, had rarely been recorded, and when they had been observed, were often misinterpreted. Thus, guidebooks refer to the 'harbour' at Appolonia, when there is no harbour, and some who should know better, still talk of Caesarea's Brechat Cleopatra as a swimming pool.

The reader who has reached thus far in my reminiscences, will have noted the pleasure which I derive from recording ancient structures on the shore-line. May I commend this activity to anyone who wishes to do his own bit of archaeological research without the necessity of digging. All that one needs is an observant eye and a willingness to get one's feet wet.

It is sometimes said that the days of the amateur are over; a statement often repeated, particularly in terms of the exploration of the Lands of the Bible. I did not believe this twenty-five years ago and now, in the light of my own experiences, I believe it even less. I have written that the early explorers had stopped at the sea's edge. I was wrong; they usually stopped much further inland and the same can be said for the majority of the archaeologists who followed them.

In the Bible Lands alone, there are thousands of miles of beaches still awaiting exploration, and for the intelligent observer, there are on these beaches the remains of thousands of years of Man's maritime history. The amateur can, with sketch pad, measuring rod and camera, set himself on a course of study that can be rewarding in the extreme. It is often overlooked that the first steps in archaeology are not 'digging' but 'observation'. The predisturbance survey is the standard prerequisite of every archaeological investigation. In the case of shoreline surveys where remains are less likely to be fully covered, results of surveys are often so revealing as to render full excavation less immediately essential. My surveys of the *piscinae* at Caesarea and Lapithos, as well as the survey of the wall and harbour at Jezirat Fara'un, were carried out entirely without excavation, producing evidence not previously recorded and the opportunity for original conclusions.

What is more, the amateur need have no fear of trespassing on the interests of the professional, for as no excavation is involved, his site would be left fully undisturbed. Any photographs or records, no matter how brief, would certainly be of value to the serious researcher. This applies particularly nowadays, when so many sites are threatened by resort developments. In the first instance, it is not necessary to identify the nature of the shore structures; indeed, it often takes much study to do just that. Just a photograph or two, a rough sketch and a few dimensions, even if they are only paced out roughly, are sufficient to start the observer on a course of absorbing study.

From time to time, friends and divers, even strangers, knowing of my interest in shoreline archaeology, send me information on places they have come across. Sometimes these are of sites that are already well-documented, but more often than not they provide fresh information on scantly studied areas. The range of subjects is extensive and embraces harbours, quays, dockyards, docking basins, slipways, ship sheds, jetties, moles and breakwaters, fishtanks, fish traps, salt pans, dye tanks and remains of seaside villas. One correspondent sent me an aerial photograph of a site that looks much like a submerged town which, as far as I am aware, is quite unknown except to the local fishermen.

My advice to the reader who shares my natural partiality for beachcombing and wishes to turn this to advantage is – observe and keep on observing; record, photograph, and enquire at the nearest museum, and you are on your way.

In an early chapter I posed the question whether biblical archaeology could ever be practised under water. I am aware of the current controversies surrounding the very subject of biblical archaeology, and do not intend to enter that arena here. What I would say, however, is that the researches that have gone on over the last twenty-five years or so, have shown quite conclusively that archaeology, both underwater and on the shorelines of the Lands of the Bible, has made, and will continue to make, important contributions to our knowledge of the biblical period and of the later periods of these fascinating lands.

In this book I have related some of my personal experiences in the Mediterranean, the Red Sea and on the shores of Israel, Cyprus and the Sinai Desert. But the story of the Bible peoples extends to the farthest shores of the Mediterranean and possibly beyond. It embraces Arabia, Egypt, the Persian Gulf, the lands and the seas of the Ancient Assyrians and the Babylonians, the lakes and rivers of these lands and the legendary countries of Cush and Punt. The ancient mariners of these times sailed their craft to the very edges of the world that they knew, and it is in their wake that the nautical archaeologist aims to travel.

Bibliography

CHAPTER 1

British Sub-Aqua Club: *Diving Manual*. London 1980.
CMAS: *The Underwater Challenge*. London 1962.
Taylor, du Plat, J.: *Marine Archaeology*. Hutchinson. London 1965.
Kirkman, J.: *Gedi, The Arab City*. Kenya Museum. 1960.

CHAPTER 2

Cohen, F.: *Red Sea Divers Guide*. Tel Aviv 1975.
Conder, C. R.: *Palestine*. George Philip. London 1891.
Conder, C. R.: *Tent Work in Palestine*. R. Bentley. London 1879.
Kinglake, A. W.: *Eothen*. London 1844.
Linder, E.: *Underwater Archaeology. A New Dimension in the Study of Israel in Antiquity*. Israel 1971.
Macaulay, R.: *The Pleasure of Ruins*. Thames and Hudson. 1953.
MacGregor, W.: *The Rob Roy on the Jordan*. John Murray. 1869.
Roberts, D.: *The Holy Land*. Day & Son. London 1855.
Robinson, E.: *Biblical Researches in Palestine*. John Murray. London 1841.
Smith, G. A.: *The Historical Geography of the Holy Land*. Hodder & Stoughton. London 1894.
Wilde, W. R.: *Wilde's Narrative*. Curry. Dublin 1840.

CHAPTER 3

Harden, D.: *The Phoenicians*. Thames & Hudson. London 1962.
Linder, E.: *A Cargo of Phoenician-Punic Figurines*. Archaeology.
Linder, E. & Flinder, A.: *Export Goddesses from the Sea*. Illustrated London News. September 1973.
Moscati, F.: *The World of the Phoenicians*. Weidenfeld & Nicholson. 1965.
Picard, G.: *Carthage*. Elek. 1956.

165

CHAPTER 4

Arconati de, G.: *Diario in Arabia Petrea*. 1872.
Aharoni, Y.: *The Land of the Bible*. London 1967.
Biek, C.: *Sinai in Arabia and of Midian*. Trubner. London 1878.
Burkhardt, J. C.: *Travels in Syria and the Holy Land*. London.
Burton, R.: *The Land of Midian Revisited*. London 1878.
Curelly, C. T.: *Researches in Sinai by Flinders Petrie*. 1906.
Flinder, A.: *The Island of Jezirat Fara'un*. International Journal of Nautical Archaeology. 1977.
Frost, H.: *The Offshore Island Harbour at Sidon etc*. International Journal of Nautical Archaeology. 1975.
Glueck, N.: *The Other Side of the Jordan*. 1940.
Glueck, N.: *Rivers in the Desert*. Weidenfeld & Nicholson. London 1959.
Glueck, N.: *Ezion Geber*. Biblical Archaeologist. 1965.
Grattan, J.: *How to Find*. BSAC. 1973.
Gordon, C. H.: *Before Columbus*. Turnstone. London 1971.
Jarvis, C. F.: *Desert & Delta*. London 1938.
Laborde, L.: *Voyage en Arabie Petree*. John Murray. London 1836.
Linder, E. & Raban, A.: *Marine Archaeology*. Cassell. London 1975.
Plowden, J. M. C. (Madam Jullien): *Once in Sinai*. Methuen. London 1940.
Pollack, A. N.: *History of the Arabs*. 1945.
Ritter, C.: *Comparative Geography of Holy Land and the Sinai Peninsula*. 1866.
Roberts, D.: *The Holy Land*. Day & Son. London 1956.
Robinson, E.: *Biblical Researches in Palestine*. John Murray. London 1887.
Rothenberg, B.: *God's Wilderness*. Thames & Hudson. London 1961.
Rothenberg, B. *Timna*. Thames & Hudson. London 1972.
Ruppell: *Ruinen auf der Insel Emrag*. 1841.
Savignac, M. R.: *Une Visite à l'île de Gray*. 1913.
Smith, G. A.: *The Historical Geography of the Holy Land*. Hodder & Stoughton. London 1894.
Tolkowsky, S.: *They Took to the Sea*. Yoseloff. London 1964.
Wellstead, J. R.: *Survey of the Gulf of Akabah*. 1838.
Woolley, C. L. & Lawrence, T. E.: *Wilderness of Zinn*. 1914.
Yadin, Y.: *The Art of Warfare in Biblical Lands*. Weidenfeld & Nicholson. London 1963.

CHAPTERS 5 AND 6

Barrow, H.: *Life of Admiral Sir Sidney Smith*. 1848.
Dichter, B.: *The Maps of Acre. An Historical Cartography*. 1973.

Bibliography

Prawer, J.: *The World of the Crusaders*. Weidenfeld & Nicholson. London 1972.

Runciman, S.: *The History of the Crusades*. Cambridge University Press. 1951.

Visnauf de, Geoffrey & Richard of Devisez: *Chronicles of the Crusades*. Bonn. 1848.

CHAPTER 7

Conder, C. R.: *Lieut. Claude R. Conder's Reports*. Palestine Exploration Fund. 1873.

Conder, C. R.: *Tent Work in Palestine*. R. Bentley. London 1879.

Flemming, N. C.: *Cities in the Sea*. NEL. London 1972.

Fritsch, C. F. & Ben-Dor I: *The Link Expedition to Israel*. Biblical Archaeologist. 1960.

Hohlfelder, R. L., Oleson, J. P., Raban, A. & Vann, R. L.: *Sebastos: Herod's Harbour at Caesarea*. The Biblical Archaeologist. 1983.

Josephus Flavius: *The War of the Jews*.

Levine, L. I.: *Roman Caesarea*. QEDAM. 1975.

Pockocke, R.: *Descriptions of the East and Some Other Countries*. 1738.

Raban, A.: *The Ancient Harbours of Caesarea Maritima*. CAHEP. 1983.

Reifenberg, A.: *Caesarea. A Study in the Decline of a Town*. IEJ. 1950.

Thomson, W. D.: *The Land and the Book*. London 1859.

CHAPTER 8

Flinder, A. & Nicolaou, K.: *Ancient Fish Tanks at Lapithos, Cyprus*. IJNA. 1976.

Flinder, A.: *A Piscina at Caesarea – A Preliminary Survey*. Israel Exploration Journal. 1976.

Forster, E. S.: *Columella II De Re Rustica* V–IX. 1954.

Hooper, D. H.: *Catto & Varro de Re Rustica*. 1934.

Schmiedt, G.: *Il Livello Antico Del Mar Tirreno*. Olschki Bologna. 1972.

CHAPTER 9

Baker, J. T.: *Tyrenian Purple. An Ancient Dye. A Modern Problem*. Endeavour. January 1974.

Epstein, J.: *The Babylonian Talmud*. Soncino Press. 1935.

Harris, H. A.: *Sport in Greece & Rome*. Thames & Hudson. London 1972.

Jidejian, N.: *Tyre Through the Ages*. Beirut 1969.

Patai, R.: *Jewish Seafaring in Ancient Times*. Jewish Quarterly Review. 1941.

Secrets of the Bible Seas

CHAPTER 10

Basch, L.: *The Athlit Ram: A Preliminary Introduction and Report:* Mariners Mirror. February 1982.
Frost, H.: *The Athlit Ram:* A Round Table Conference at Haifa University. IJNA. February 1982.
Linder, E. & Ramon, Y.: *The Athlit Ram.* Archaeology. 1981.
Raban, A.: *The Finds from the Undersea Site at Hof HaCarmel.* Sefunim. 1969–71.
Rottenberg, B.: Timna. *Valley of the Biblical Copper Mines.* Thames & Hudson. 1972.
Steffy, J. R.: *The Athlit Ram: A Preliminary Investigation of its Structure.* Mariners Mirror. August 1983.

CHAPTER 11

Raban, A.: *The Shipwreck off Sharm-el-Sheikh.* Archaeology. April 1971.

CHAPTERS 12 AND 13

Fritsch, C. F. & Ben-Dor I: *The Link Expedition to Israel.* Biblical Archaeologist. 1960.
Kitchener, H. H.: Paper in the Palestine Exploration Fund Quarterly. 1877.
Linder, E.: *La Ville Phenicienne D'Athlit A-T-Elle Eu L'Un Des Plus Anciens Ports Artificiels de Mediterranee.* Archaeologia. July 1967.
MacGregor, W.: *The Rob Roy on the Jordan.* John Murray. London 1869.
Raban, A.: *Some Archaeological Evidence for Ancient Maritime Activities at Dor.* Sefunim. 1981.

FURTHER READING ON MARINE ARCHAEOLOGY

Bascom, W.: *Deep Water, Ancient Ships.* David & Charles. London 1976.
Bass, G. F.: *A History of Seafaring.* Thames & Hudson. London 1972.
Bass, G. F.: *Archaeology Beneath the Sea.* Walker. New York 1975.
Bass, G. F.: *Archaeology Under Water.* Thames & Hudson. London 1966.
Bass, G. F.: *Cape Gelidonya. A Bronze Age Shipwreck.* Archaeology. 1967.
Casson, L.: *Ships & Seamanship in the Ancient World.* London 1971.
Frost, H.: *Under the Mediterranean.* Routledge & Kegan Paul. London 1963.
Linder, E. & Raban, A.: *Marine Archaeology.* Cassell. London 1975.

168

Bibliography

McKee, A.: *History Under the Sea*. Hutchinson. London 1968.

Marsden, P. *The Wreck of the Amsterdam*. Hutchinson. London 1975.

Martin, C.: *Full Fathom Five. The Wrecks of the Spanish Armada*. Chatto & Windus. London 1975.

Marx, R. F.: *Port Royal Rediscovered*. NEL. London 1973.

Muckleroy, K.: *Maritime Archaeology*. London 1979.

Muckleroy, K.: *Archaeology Under Water. An Atlas of the World's Submerged Sites*. McGraw. London 1980.

Parker, A. J.: *Ancient Shipwrecks of the Mediterranean and the Roman Provinces*. British Archaeological Review. 1980.

Rule, M.: *The Mary Rose. The Excavation and Raising of Henry VIII's Flagship*. Souvenir Press. London 1982.

Throckmorton, P.: *Shipwrecks and Archaeology*. Gollancz. London 1970.

Wilkes, B. St J.: *Nautical Archaeology: A Handbook*. David & Charles. 1971.

In addition to the above, the *International Journal of Nautical Archaeology* is recommended. It is published quarterly by the Academic Press.

Index

Index

Roman 52, 105
Procopius (of Gaza) 109
Ptolemais (*former name of* Acre) 91
Pulteoli Market 117
purple dye 126–8

Raban, Avner 111, 136, 144, 149
  and the Acre artefacts 136–7
Ras Muhammed (Sinai) 142
Red Sea 61
Rob Roy on the Jordan, The (MacGregor) 27, 157–8
Robinson, E. 27
Romans 25, 91, 101, 108, 114, 128
  aqueducts 102
  coins 102, 136
  coral dealing 129
  pottery 105, 155
Rothenberg, Benno 49, 63, 64

Salammbo (near Carthage) 38
Salammbo (Flaubert) 39
Santorin (Aegean) 124
Scillias (Greek diver) 129
Sebastos harbour 102, 110
  see also Caesarea
sharks 46, 128
Sharm el Sheik 47
Shave Zion 30–41, 119, 138
Shaw, Joseph 24–5, 26
Shikmona site 135–7
shoreline surveys 163
Sidon 28, 40, 61
Simi (Aegean) 124
Sinai Desert 43, 45, 52
snorkelling 136
Smith, Captain William Sidney 88–90
Solomon, King 39, 61, 126
sponges (sea creatures) 124–5
stone
  Caesarea blocks 105
  cyclopic 92–4
stratigraphy 59, 110, 162
Stratos Tower 102
  see also Caesarea
syenite 109
Syracuse 39
Syrian/African Rift Valley 47

Taba 44
Tabgha (Galilee) 158–9
Talmud 109
  divers' legend 129–30
  purple dye 127–8
Tanit, Goddess
  Enigmatic sign of 30, 31
  figurines 12, 35, 41
Tantura (village) 149
Taylor, Joan du Plat, *see* du Plat Taylor, Joan
Tekhelet purple dye 126–8
Tel Aviv 101
telephones, undersea 115
Tell el-Kheleifeh (Aqaba) 64
terracotta 120
  figurines 29, 35
tesserae 121
Theodora coins 136
Tiberius 26, 155, 160
tidal waves 131
Timna Valley 63, 64
Tophet 38–9
Tower of Flies (Acre) 92–100
  Greek fire cylinders 99–100
  legends 92
  stone 92–5
  and the Third Crusade 96–100
Turks 45, 95, 100
Tyre 28, 31, 40, 41, 61, 130
  dye factories 128
  Iron Age walls 153

Ugaritic text 92
underwater archaeology, *see* archaeology, underwater
underwater metal detectors 54

Venus figurines 136, 138
Vespasian 108
Vitruvius: on architecture 111

War of the Jews, The (Josephus) 102, 155
Wheeler, Sir Mortimer 17–18, 161
Woolley, Sir Leonard 50, 58, 81

Yamm (sea-god) 92

Acknowledgements

Pages 65 (top), 80: The Israel Maritime Museum, Haifa. Pages 72, 73: Luis Marden, National Geographic Society. Pages 69 (bottom), 77, 78 (top and bottom), 79: Joseph Galilee. All other photographs courtesy of Alexander Flinder.

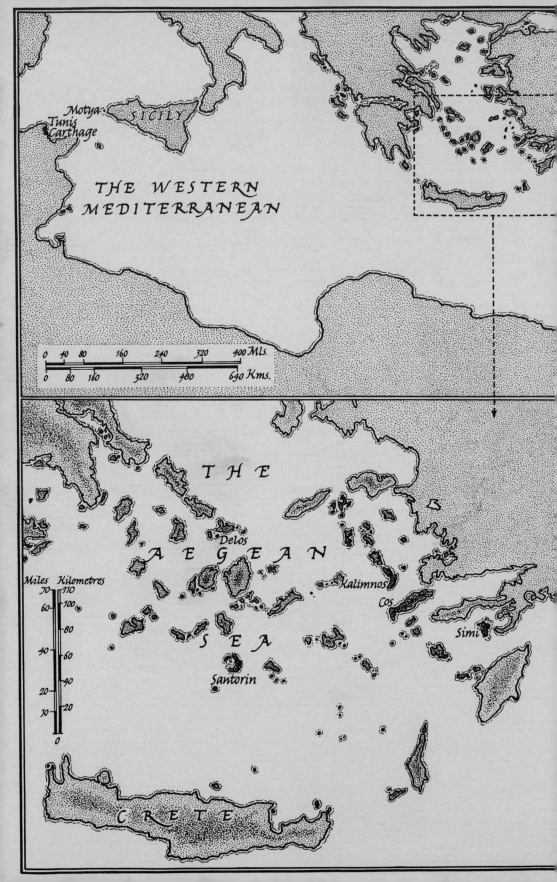

Motya
Tunis
Carthage

SICILY

THE WESTERN
MEDITERRANEAN

0 40 80   160   240   320   400 Mls.
0   80 160   320   480   640 Kms.

THE

A E G E A N

Delos

Kalimnos

Cos

Simi

S E A

Santorin

Miles Kilometres
70   110
60   100
        80
40   60
20   40
10   20
      0

CRETE